MY LIFE OF REVOLT

THE AUTHOR

My Life of
REVOLT

BY

DAVID KIRKWOOD

M.P. J.P.

WITH FOREWORDS BY THE RT. HON.
WINSTON S. CHURCHILL C.H. M.P.
AND THE RT. HON.
GEORGE LANSBURY M.P.

GEORGE G. HARRAP & CO. LTD.
LONDON   BOMBAY   SYDNEY

TO
MY WIFE

REF

B

KIRKWOOD

First published November 1935
by GEORGE G. HARRAP & CO. LTD.
182 High Holborn, London, W.C.1
Reprinted November 1935
Copyright. All rights reserved

Made in Great Britain. Printed by Morrison & Gibb, Ltd.,
London and Edinburgh

FOREWORD

BY THE RT. HON.

WINSTON S. CHURCHILL, C.H., M.P.

DAVID KIRKWOOD has so many friends of all parties in the House of Commons and at large in the country that this engaging account of his pugnacious career will receive a warm welcome. Every one thinks him a grand fellow, if handled the right way. The ' if,' however, is very important. Without it there must be, as his chapter-headings imply, storms, hurricanes, and, I will add, typhoons. In a revealing passage of his book he reflects upon his conflicts with the British Government on points of ' principle ' in the grim height of the War, and how he held stern parley with the military and civil authorities, and how decently they treated him. " What a country ! Imagine such a series of incidents and such a scene in any other country ! It is incredible. Had I been anywhere but in Britain, I should have been quietly dispatched as a nuisance or a traitor ! Nuisance I may have been. Traitor I never was.

" Sometimes some of my colleagues wonder when I speak of this land in the way I do. I have most reason to know that it is in very truth the land of the brave and the free. . . ."

This book is valuable for the picture it gives of

the feelings and thoughts of the radically minded wage-earners. Their sturdy independence, their mood of political revolt, their strong suspicion that they are being 'got at' and put upon, their super-developed sense of injustice, their hatred of snobbery and affectation, their readiness to use their rights as citizens to the full, their innate conviction that one man is as good as another, or better—these traits show themselves on every page. Side by side with them the author exposes his deep love of Scotland and his lively realization of all that British liberty means to the mass of our island folk.

David Kirkwood and the strong type he represents are the natural foes of tyranny. Gripped in the iron regimentations of the Continent, they would resist with an indomitable, or at the worst desperate, tenacity. Many of his readers have disapproved of his views and actions in the past, and will probably do so in the future. But should the life and freedom of our race again be called in question we shall all find ourselves together heart and hand.

WINSTON S. CHURCHILL

FOREWORD

BY THE RT. HON.

GEORGE LANSBURY, M.P.

DAVID KIRKWOOD has asked me to write a brief foreword to this book.

David is one of my colleagues to whom it is difficult to say " No." On this occasion I gladly say " Yes," because he is one of the most hard-working colleagues both in and out of the House of Commons, and one who when he disagrees with you does so in a kindly, good-humoured, tolerant manner. He is always sure of an audience when speaking in Parliament, and at question time is a real terror to Ministers whom he wishes to cross-examine. Like most Scots politicians, he is a merciless, persistent heckler ; once he has made up his mind to pursue a question neither the over-whelming shouts of his fellow-Members nor the gentle reproofs of the Speaker can put him down. Although this is the case, he has learned from experience just how far he can go, but, what is far more important in Parliament, he has discovered how to use words and the rules of order in such a manner as to enable him to pursue a subject to the utmost limits. Of course, he has graduated in that most excellent of schools, experience. He did not find the path of a heckler very rosy when first he crossed swords in wordy warfare with Mr Speaker Whitley.

I like to remember him during the days of the

War, a prisoner in Edinburgh, banished from home and kindred because, no matter what the authorities thought of him, he wished to help the men who were fighting in that hell-begotten struggle in France and Belgium. I met him and his fellow-prisoners, and endeavoured to secure their freedom by getting pledges as to their future behaviour. I forget what was the end of my efforts, but I remember David, dour and determined, quite clear as to what he wanted, quietly and persistently turning down every suggestion of compromise.

You will find in this book the full story of muddle and mismanagement which brainy men and women, accustomed to organizing for private profit, created when striving to produce munitions for the War, and you will also learn how men like David and his friends, quite untrained in the ways of Capitalism, were able to render services to the Government. I am glad he has told us a little of John Wheatley, whose premature death was a loss not only to our Labour Movement, but to the world.

I wish the book a very big circulation. It should be in every public and private library, so that the public may know at first hand what a good specimen of a man David Kirkwood, beloved of cartoonists, really is.

The audiences which crowd to listen to him from John o' Groats to Land's End know him as a bonnie fighter on behalf of the people to whom he is proud to belong. People who only read of him in party newspapers cannot without further knowledge understand what a tireless worker and servant of the nation he really is.

GEORGE LANSBURY

CONTENTS

ILLUSTRATIONS

CHAPTER I

The Kirkwoods of Parkhead

I HAVE often heard my father say to my mother : "Never heed, Jeanie, we'll win through yet."

"Winning through" did not mean achieving any high ambition. There was no prospect or thought of "the glittering prizes of life" to entice him to special effort. "Winning through" meant surviving, not being starved, not being homeless, not being in debt. It meant, above all, not being thrown on the parish. To be forced to accept parish relief was to be cast into the bottomless pit of humiliation. "The glorious privilege of being independent" was no mere poet's fancy. It was the very marrow of life. To receive aught without fair return was to lose self-respect. The folk from whom I am sprung would give without grudge ; they never learned to receive with grace. They were shy, as most Scots are. Sometimes their very shyness would make them aggressive, more to conquer their own shyness than to overcome another person. They were sentimental, as all Scots are. But, by one of the peculiar tricks of human nature, they were ashamed of their own emotions. In a crowd, they would wallow in

sentiment. They would become almost tearful
as they sang of " My ain kind dearie O," but they
would think shame to speak tenderly to their wives
and children in public.   Nevertheless, they were a
remarkable people.   In all his life my father never
earned as much as thirty shillings a week.   His
father had never earned twenty, and his grandfather's wage varied between twelve and fifteen.
Yet they were men of knowledge and culture and
character—aye, well put on, and, in their way,
notables in the district.   The district was Parkhead,
a village of five thousand people, on the eastern
boundary of the City of Glasgow.   It was still a
village when I was born, a village of hand-loom
weavers, whose houses held the loom on the ground
floor and the living apartments overhead.   My
people were not weavers.   The weavers were a
cut above them.   They were labourers, big, strong,
hefty men, strong-featured, and noted for their
black hair and dark eyes.   How long they had
lived in the district I do not know, but " there
was aye a Kirkwood in Parkheid " was as familiar
as the Highland phrase :   " There was aye a pier
at Lochranza."

Many years ago, when I was in one of my
tantrums with Sir William Beardmore of Parkhead Forge, he made a remark about Parkhead
Forge being the life of Parkhead.   The remark
made me blaze.   I said :

" Let me tell you, Sir William, that there were
Kirkwoods in Parkheid afore the Beardmores were
heard tell o', and there'll be Kirkwoods in Parkheid
when the name o' Beardmore is a thing o' the past."

That was a statement of fact. It was also a prophecy, to be fulfilled all too soon, to my great sorrow.

My great-grandfather was sufficient of a notable to have a nickname which is still remembered in the district. The women knew him as " Auld Jock " Kirkwood. To the men he was " Ruble " Kirkwood. He was a carter. The City of Glasgow had resolved to rear a monument in the Glasgow Green in honour of Lord Nelson. It took the form of a massive stone pillar on a massive stone plinth. The massive stone monuments of that day were not solid stone. The retaining walls were stone, but the internals were made of rubble and cement. For months my great-grandfather carted loads of rubble from Parkhead to Glasgow Green to fill up the cavern of the monument. Hence the nickname, " Ruble " Kirkwood.

" Ruble " Kirkwood was a man of strong character and, like all the folk of weaving centres, he was an ardent Radical. There seems to have been a subtle association between weaving and Radicalism in Scotland. In such places as Bridgeton in Glasgow, Paisley, and Kilbarchan, the people were conservative in their liberalism. Paisley was Radical before the Reform Act of 1832, and has never elected a Conservative to Parliament in its history. It may be that these men and women, weaving patterns of cloth, wove at the same time patterns of life. Or it may be that the work, although intricate, became automatic and allowed the mind to browse in the meadows of thought. Did not David Livingstone learn Latin from a text-book propped up in front of him as he wove the cloth? Whatever the cause, these old weavers were Radicals, and, like all Radicals, they dearly loved an argument. Unlike their English cousins, they could all read and write. The old Church Parish Schools taught their pupils how to learn and, long before education was made compulsory by law, it had become a necessity by tradition. To be illiterate was to lack dignity, and dignity was, and is, to the Scot as essential a feature as it was to the Roman.

Like his great-grandson, " Ruble " Kirkwood had trouble with the authorities and the military. It arose out of a right-of-way. Rights-of-way share with theology the distinction of being the most fertile cause of trouble in Scotland. For centuries, the bonnie banks of the Clyde, above Glasgow, were the favourite walking and courting area of the district. A Glasgow distiller, Harvey by name, bought the lands of West Thorn, around which, with many a bend and turn, the river twined on its way to the beautiful Horse-shoe Bend. In times of spate the river overflowed the banks and flooded the low-lying lands of West Thorn. Harvey employed an army of men to deepen the river. With the material of the trenching, he reared a high embankment like the defences of a Roman camp. On this embankment he laid down a carriage-way, two miles in length. It is still there.

At the west end of the estate Harvey built a mansion-house. At the east end he reared a heavy wall of stone, four feet thick and fifteen feet high from the embankment to the river. This wall blocked the banks o' Clyde. The young men and maidens sighed at the closing of the lovers' walk. The older men saw in it an infringement of the Rights of Man. A question of principle was involved. Whenever a Scotsman thinks a question of principle is involved he makes ready for action.

The French Revolution had not been in vain. The tocsin was sounded. Armed with pickaxes, crowbars, and shovels, the weavers of Parkhead, Tollcross, and Bridgeton marched out to the wall. It was toughly built, but crowbars and picks can work wonders. One by one the great stones were levered up and tumbled off into the river, each victory being greeted with cheers for the Rights of Man. The police arrived in full panoply, but the crowd was so dense that they could not approach the wall and the workers. Foiled, they reported the occurrence to headquarters. Headquarters reported to the barracks, built to hold the weavers in subjection at the time of the Reform Bill agitation. The dragoons galloped to the spot. They were too late. The wall was no more. The Rights of Man had been vindicated.

The affair led to a trial in the High Court of Justiciary. The charge was that of " forming part of a disorderly mob and inciting to riot "—a phrase with which I also became fairly familiar ! The court upheld the Rights of Man. The people's cause triumphed.

The wall was rebuilt ; the lovers' walk was left

free ; one of the loveliest paths in the West of Scotland was preserved for the people. The carriage drive, known as Harvey's Dyke, remains. The wall may still be traced, but there is little left of the beauty of the scene. Industry came to Parkhead. The blast-furnaces couped their clinker on the wildflowers and the gorse, and made of it a scene of desolation and despair. Those old weavers set a higher store on the beauties of Nature than the industrialists who superseded them.

I often think that the unity of these weaver folk has never been equalled. They were a corporate body. They knew each other. They chose their wives from their own circle. They were all poor. They had to work, man and wife, long, long hours for an existence. But there was a fine spirit among them. They had co-operative schemes that have not been equalled by the vast co-operative societies of later days. In Parkhead the weavers formed the Parkhead Economic Society. They pledged themselves to buy all their goods from the Society. At the end of every six months' trading, there took place the great event, known as the " coont-oot." Stock was taken, the accounts were audited. The surplus was divided among the members equally. Unlike the modern co-operative dividend, which is based on purchases, the " coont-oot " was based on membership. The poor old lone woman with only a few shillings a week got her share, equal to that of the man with a good wage and several sons working. They bought according to their means. They shared equally in the surplus. The surplus was distributed not in cash, but in goods—meal and flour, blankets and boots.

For years the system worked. Then strangers began to filter into the district, to the mills and the pits and the foundries. They were fly. The communal spirit was of no interest to them. They joined the Society to share in the divide, but they bought only the goods that were cheaper than they could buy elsewhere. The Society collapsed. The multiple shop and the Co-operative Society fought for their custom and ushered in the Age of Woolworth.

My great-grandfather had a large family, but only one of his sons interests me. He was my grandfather, a tall, strapping man, a regular Black Kirkwood. His name was David, "Auld Davie" Kirkwood. When he was a boy a man, Gray, found coal at Parkhead and sank a shaft. He called his pit the Caroline Pit, after Queen Caroline, not so much in honour of the unattractive Queen as in contempt for her royal husband. It was a wonderful pit, the finest in lay-out and equipment in the world. Neither women nor children were employed in it. Young David was entered as a labourer on the opening day. He remained until the day it closed, fifty-two years later. Then he crossed over to Beardmore's Forge, where he worked until he was eighty-two years of age.

The "Karleen" Pit was closed; not because it was worked out. It was closed on a question of principle, which is often another name for pride. The proprietor was a man of invention. In order to keep a clean pit, he had installed the finest pumping machinery known at that time. It was costly. The water seemed limitless. After years of seeking the reason for the presence of so much water, he discovered that he was pumping the water from seven other pits extending as far away as Airdrie, twelve miles out. This was too much to ask of a man. He invited the other owners to a conference, at which he pointed out that he was bearing the cost of pumping all their pits as well as his own. Would they share the cost with him? They would not.

" Then," he said, " I shall stop pumping."

They laughed at the idea. They knew he was a rich man. They knew the Caroline Pit was highly remunerative, notwithstanding the cost of pumping. They knew he could not compel them to share the cost. He would never stop pumping. It would mean closing the pit.

They refused to share. On the day he received their decision, Gray gave all his men their pay and told them to look for jobs elsewhere. Then he walked away from the pit and never came back to it again.

The pit-owners had made a bad mistake. Every pit became flooded. They were forced to instal pumping machinery. The Caroline was abandoned.

" Auld Davie " Kirkwood, my grandfather, was a man of great dignity. Although very poor in this world's gear, he was proud in spirit and rich in character. He was a happy soul. He faced the world with a smile. Nothing could

THE LAIRD AND MY GRANDFATHER

"RUBLE" KIRKWOOD

8

disturb him, nothing could depress him. He was never known to show anger and never bore a grudge. To him all manner of men came for counsel. The laird, calling for his rent, would share with him a dram and a crack. The aged came to him with their cares and the young with their dreams. To the last, he retained a youthful mind, and, talking in broad Doric, which is not the same as the modern " Glesca " accent, he would talk with young and old of politics and literature and the doings of the olden times, illustrating his arguments with quotations from the Bible and Robert Burns.

He was one of the best-informed men in the district, largely due to the fact that it was to him that the weekly newspaper was delivered. He read it through from beginning to end. The news-paper cost $4\frac{1}{2}d.$ and was bought by the Club of Readers, who contributed one half-penny a fort-night for the purchase. They appointed a 'reader,' an excellent exercise in articulation. When the newspaper arrived, the Club met in an eicht-loom shop. The news was read and discussed.

Young men were welcomed to the Club as listeners. As a result of listening to the mature discussion, the young became well informed on the events of the day and the ' principles ' by which they were judged. So keenly interested were the young men that often there was not room for them all. It was from this employment of dialectic that some of the young men formed a club of their own, which met at seven in the morning to study logic ! No workman, of course, could go to such a class, for they had to begin their own work at six in the morning.

Whenever I see Whistler's portrait of Thomas Carlyle in the Glasgow Art Gallery, I think of my grandfather in his old age, dignified, pensive, and warm, a splendid specimen of that Scottish character which has become a legend. Their manners did not lack the repose that marks the caste of Vere de Vere. They were poor, but they were aristocrats. Their pedigree was not known, but it was long and honourable.

CHAPTER II

My Father

UNLIKE my grandfather, my father was a serious man. On a question of principle—and almost everything could become a question of principle—he was adamant. He was of the stuff of the Covenanters. He would have gone to the stake for an idea, if he thought it right. It would never have occurred to him that he might possibly be wrong, any more than it would occur to him that he might possibly be late for his work in the morning. That never happened once in his life. He was as regular as clockwork.

At five o'clock in the morning a horn sounded in a workshop near our home. My father was always half-way down the stairs, probably on the exact step, every morning when that horn blew. Such a practice was an example of the mania for self-reliance which was characteristic of his generation. To be on the same step of the stair when the horn blew meant much thought and anxiety every morning in order to anticipate the sounding of the horn by a few seconds. He could have kept his mind at peace if he had made a rule to leave the house when the horn blew. It would have meant only ten seconds in time. But in character it would have meant sloppiness, dependence on an external instrument. No external instrument should mould him into mental slackness. No matter what he had been doing the night before, nor how late he had been, nor whether or not he felt up to the mark, not once in his life was he a minute behind time. He was as regular in his return home. My mother could confidently prepare his supper for seven o'clock in the evening. He would be there.

He had a passion for cleanliness. He never smoked. He spent no money on himself, except that occasionally in the evening he would take a dram. Then all his seriousness and austerity would disappear. He would laugh and sing in a deep bass voice :

> O' a' the airts the win' can blaw
>   I dearly like the west.
> For there the bonnie lassie lives,
>   The lassie I lo'e best ;
> There wild-woods grow and rivers row
>   And mony a hill between.
> Baith day and nicht my fancy's flicht
>   Is ever wi' my Jean.

As he reached the last line, he would look archly across to my mother and say, " Never heed, Jeanie, we'll win through yet," and wave his hand as if he owned the town.

The Scots share with the Jews a sense of mystery with regard to names, and can express their emotions in the tone with which they speak a name. If I had ever heard my father call my mother " Jean," I should have known there was trouble between them. When he called her " Jeanie," I knew all was well.

He was a strange creature. He was a labourer. He should have been a farmer. Everything associated with the soil, with animals, birds, and trees, made a strong appeal to him. To him a bird was a living thing, a singing thing, a mating thing ; a horse was a creature of power and beauty ; a plough was as mathematical an instrument as a set-square.

He would look at a well-ploughed field, wave his hand, cock his head on one side and say to me : " Whit d'ye think o' that, my cullan ? Is that no' bonnie ? "

Whenever he spoke of the soil and things associated with the soil, he used the Doric, as he did when he was moved. Otherwise he used English, which he spoke with a rhythmic eloquence.

One of his great joys was to take me walking on a Saturday afternoon and have a talk with a farmer or a ploughman. To me these walks were a most joyous experience, though my father would walk me till I was fit to drop. Even as a child, I preferred walking with my father to playing with other children. We were monarchs of the world. He knew every bird and would talk to them in wooing terms, then speak some lines of poetry, telling me the author. I was so young that I cannot now remember the exact words, nor have I his natural eloquence, but I can give an impression.

Seeing crows in a cornfield, he would stop and, pointing them out to me, would begin :

"There ye are, my cullan, five o' the black beauties. Ha, ha, ye mischiefs, sinfu' thievers that ye are, robbin' the puir fairmer o' his corn ! He'll get ye yet wi' his gun, an' then whit a cloud o' black feathers there will be !

"There were twa corbies sat on a stane,
Bonnie St Johnstone stands on Tay."

If a lark soared singing to the sky, he would stop and begin :

"There ye are, my cullan, the bonnie lark. Sing on, ye bonnie warbler, bird thou never wert ; if I had hauf yer happiness, I'd sing wi' ye, high into the blue, blue silence o' heaven till the angels wud hearken. 'Hail to thee, blithe spirit.' There's a wonderful poem beginning that way, my cullan, written by the poet Keats, an' there's a fine song that goes : 'Hark, hark, the lark at heaven's gate sings.' A bonnie bird it is, that nests on the ground and sings in the sky."

So, too, when we met acquaintances, he would talk on equal terms with minister, doctor, ploughman, or dairymaid. And afterwards he would say : "That's Mary, my cullan, Mary Campbell, same name as Robert Burns's Hielan' Mary, puir lass. Mary, Queen o' Scots, had four Marys as her maids-in-waiting.

"Yestreen the Queen had four Marys,
This nicht she'll hae but three,
There was Mary Beaton and Mary Seaton
And Mary Carmichael and me."

Whenever the spring-time peeped through the

fogs of winter, my father watched for the daisies. He would come in from his work, holding a daisy in his hand, and even before he cleaned himself he would call :

" See, Jeanie, my lass, she's here, the wee daisy. We'll win through yet ! "

Then, standing in the kitchen, with the daisy in his hand, he would recite, in the Doric, Robert Burns's *Ode to a Daisy* :

> Wee, modest, crimson-tipped flow'r,
> Thou's met me in an evil hour,
> For I maun crush amang the stoure
>   Thy slender stem.
> To save thee noo is past my pow'r,
>   Thou bonnie gem.

But his favourite poem was Gray's *Elegy in a Country Churchyard*, to which he referred always by the full title. This poem was part of his daily vocabulary and, by hearing him repeat stanzas of it so often, I grew to know it by heart without having read it.

It is strange to me that a man who knew so much of poetry, the songs and the ballads, never to my knowledge mentioned Shakespeare. It may be that the antagonism which existed in Scotland against the theatre and everything associated with it excluded Shakespeare from general knowledge. Or it may be that the Scots, who are the most sentimental race on earth, found their thoughts more completely expressed in lyrics and songs of Nature. At the Fair Holiday my father would set out with a few shillings, carrying neither bag nor satchel, and tramp into the Highlands by Aberfoyle to the Trossachs, sleeping in a farmer's byre or a shepherd's shieling.

This great, powerful man, over six feet in height and weighing sixteen stone, was a labourer. He had started in the Caroline Pit as a boy. When the pit closed, he went to a weaving-mill, where he worked for thirty-six years. He began as a labourer wheeling a barrow. He rose to be winding-master at the princely wage of twenty-eight shillings a week.

I am sure he knew that he might have been something more important, though he never mentioned it. He was a great reader, a politician, a prose poet, and a natural mathematician. The manager of the mill has told me that, whenever the counting-house was in difficulty with figures, my father would be called into the office. The problem would be explained to him and, almost before the cashier had gained his breath, my father would give the solution. He worked it out by mental arithmetic. Then he had to explain how he worked it, step by step. The explanation was set down on paper and checked. My father was never once found to be wrong. I inherited nothing of this gift.

My father read widely. He had two heroes, Robert Burns and Sir Walter Scott. He revered them. To hear them called " Rabbie " and " Wattie " made him grue. The poems and songs of Robert Burns he knew by heart. His philosophy he regarded as the universal message to mankind. Robert Burns he compared with the Psalmist David.

" Men o' the soil they were, my cullan, and of
the open field ; where secrets are as fully revealed
by a drap o' dew on a blade o' grass as by the
limitless constellations o' the heavens. They were
baith singers an' they were baith sinners, wi' the
same sinning. They were baith members o' a race
that was faur doon the brae, an' by each o' them
was the nation set high amang the nations o' the
world. An' the baith o' them, in raising their ain
people, spak' tae the world. One cam' to be the
national King o' the Jews an' the ither the national
hero o' the Scots. If ye learn the Psalms o' David
and the poems o' Robert Burns, ye'll hae a thocht
ready for every incident, grave or gay, that may
come to ye in life."

I can still hear his deep, resonant voice rolling
out the comparison.

There was a serious eloquence in him when he
spoke. Indeed, he was serious in all his ways.
He was serious in his political views, so serious that
he left Gladstone on the question of Home Rule
for Ireland. It gave him a sair heart, but he said :
" Fidelity to a person must not override fidelity to
a principle."

Perhaps there was rather much ' principle ' in
his make-up. There are men who, by seeing a
principle in a molehill, transform it into a mountain.
Then it blocks their view. One of life's difficulties
is to estimate the real importance of a subject, and
not to make a matter of conscience out of a thing
which is only a matter of opinion. A man may
change an opinion and feel he has gained knowledge, but, when he has to retract what he has

made a matter of conscience, he is apt to feel that he has lost self-respect. Half of the religious squabbles of Scotland have arisen from a misunderstanding of the difference between conscience and opinion. It is largely a habit. It is also a form of conceit. It has given to the world a glorious company of martyrs, but it has made many martyrs for causes which were not glorious.

I must confess that I inherited some of that temperament from my father. How could it be otherwise? Our childish ears were full of stories of Scotland, her heroes and her martyrs, the stories of the Scottish Chiefs and Scottish Covenanters, their determination, their unbending resoluteness, their dourness. It was as if uncompromising adherence to a cause was the virtue, irrespective of whether the cause was just or not.

Names had in their sound a ring of obstinate resistance and fidelity. Sir Walter Scott had wrought this name-power to a great height— Ettrick and Teviotdale, Eskdale and Liddesdale, Glenorchy, Kilchurn, Glenstrae, and Glenlyon. So in the songs of the '45 Jacobite Rebellion we learned to feel the unyielding granite of Cameron and Clanranald, Morrison and MacGregor.

If I had inherited with my father's dourness some of the sweet, kindly, winsome nature of my mother, I should have saved myself and other people a mighty lot of trouble. But then I should not have been myself, and no one would ever have asked me to write this story of my life.

My father's father was a handsome old man. My mother's mother was as near a witch as ever you saw. I remember her in her old age, dark and swarthy as a gipsy, with black eyes glowing above a hooked nose. Her mouth was hard and determined. She had been through the fire of tribulation in her young days, when her weaver folk were starved into the mills. She worked night and day and thought everybody should do the same. As she worked, she talked to herself. At an advanced age, she worked through the whole of Friday nights, washing out the shop of a grocer, polishing the counters, the brass scales and chains, arranging the jars and tins and all the paraphernalia, so that when Saturday morning came the whole place was spick-and-span for the day of great trading. For this she received one shilling and sixpence at the hands of her niece, Belle Colquhoun.

Belle Colquhoun was a character. She was the kind of domestic servant and retainer that we read about in books. As a girl she had entered the employment of a man, Robert Watson, a licensed grocer and builder. He was rich. Within a few years of her coming to the house, Mrs Watson died, leaving two young children. Belle spread her covering wings over the brood. She reared them both, as well as their father, and a splendid job she made of it. She would have died for them.

The father married, as his second wife, a woman of beautiful character. Instead of surrendering her charges, Belle added her to the brood and she became another child to Belle. In process of time four more sons and a daughter came to the house. Belle bossed the whole show. Even when the family was grown up and exceedingly prosperous, Belle treated them all as bairns, directing them from their rising up in the morning till their going to bed at night. Not one member of the family, coming home late at night or in the wee sma' oors ayont the twal', but found Belle waiting with a " Noo, laddie, awa' till yer bed or ye'll be sweart [1] to rise the morn." A thrifty woman, she had saved from her scanty wages a few pounds which, in her will, she bequeathed equally among the wealthy men and women who had been her ' children.' They expended it all on a fine memorial stone over her grave.

I am sure that if Ian Maclaren had known my people he would have found in Parkhead a hundred stories as good as any of those he found *Beside the Bonnie Brier Bush*.

My father was a strong supporter of the Church, though he seldom mentioned religion. He took it for granted. Like a good Radical, he was a United Presbyterian. How far away seem those ecclesiastical divisions : Church of Scotland, Free Church, United Presbyterian Church, Reformed Presbyterian Church, Evangelical Union, and all the rest ! Robert Burns had exploded most of their absurdities in his satires, but the antagonism had taken new forms. In my childhood they were not only ecclesiastical, but social distinctions. The Church of Scotland, called the Established Church or the Parish Church or the Auld Kirk, was the resort of the rich and conservative. They looked down on the members of the Free Church,

[1] Disinclined.—ED.

who were evangelical and Puritans, as outcasts. The Free Kirkers in their turn looked upon the Auld Kirkers as misguided or as sinners against the light. The United Presbyterians, who emphasized the social implications of religion, went on their own way. Now they are all one. The Church of Scotland has brought her wandering children back to the ancestral home, and no one seems to be one whit better or worse.

Judged by the standards of to-day, life for the poor held few surprises. Births, marriages, and deaths, the Glasgow Fair and " the New Year," were the chief excitements. But none of them caused more pother than the annual pastoral visit of the minister. Due notice of so momentous an event was given from the pulpit. And then, what a cleansing and scrubbing of floor and deal table ; what instruction to the children in the rules of good manners ; what practising beforehand as to how we were to conduct such a performance ! The coming of the minister was the only occasion on which my mother appeared conscious of her poverty.

" If we jist had a parlour and cud ask him ben the room," she would say ; or, as she scrubbed the floor : " If only we had a bit waxcloth."

To have waxcloth on the bare wooden floor was the ambition of every woman who was houseproud. I never heard linoleum mentioned and, as for carpets, they were associated in my mind with the fairy-tales of Oriental splendour and the mansions of the rich.

So deep is tradition, that even my father was shy in the presence of the minister. As a general rule, he was easy of speech, but in the presence of the minister he became reserved. It was not due to the fact that the minister was ' college-bred,' though my people had so deep a respect for knowledge that the man of the College was regarded as an authority. ' College-bred ' was an ancient phrase meaning a graduate of the University. For centuries the University of Glasgow was known officially as " the College of Glasgow " and, though moderns talk of " the 'Varsity," the artisans, who are much more conservative in everything but politics, still refer to it as " the College."

The real truth is that my father did not like the minister, which is the same thing as saying that he did not admire him. They were both proud men, but there are variations in pride.

It happened that the manse connected with the church was in a district which had once been the countryside and was now no longer so salubrious. It was ' doon by the ree '—that is, near the colliers' rows. When the minister was called to the church, he refused point-blank to live in the manse among the colliers. All his predecessors had lived there and reared their generally numerous families in the fine big house. The man from Campbeltown *via* Stornoway would have none of it. The congregation were forced to lease a house for him in the better-class area. As they were all poor folk and the church was supported by their contributions, this expense was a heavy burden. My father held the view that the minister was "cursed wi' faus Hielan' pride."

My father had a hero among the ministers, the Reverend Norman MacLeod of the Barony. Whenever his name was mentioned—and that was very often, for he was a mighty man in Israel—my father would say : " A thoughtful man, yon ; a thinker, an original thinker and full of power." He liked to go to the Barony. He would have liked to go more often than he did, but a congregation was thirled [1] to a church, and no member liked, on meeting the minister, to be greeted with :

" I did not see you at church on Sabbath—I hope no family distress prevented you."

It was unusual in my young days for those of the labouring class to go to church. The church was regarded by them as a place for the " weel aff folk wi' guid claes." The church regarded itself in that light and provided ' missions ' for the poor who could not afford seat-rents.

My father and mother were an exception. They went to church with perfect regularity and they wore their guid claes. I don't know how it was done, but my father, with a wage of less than twenty shillings a week, set out on a Sabbath morning in a good suit of clothes and a silk hat, with my mother in a black dress and bonnet and an umbrella. And they both wore elastic-sided boots of amazing polish. For the House of God, everything had to be of the best. Nothing haphazard or second-best was permitted. However

---

[1] Bound, as a farmer was bound to a mill—that is, bound to have his corn ground at a certain mill.—ED.

we might look during the week, we had to go to church spotlessly clean, clothes brushed, boots blackened, neck and ears polished with soap. The church was the Sanctuary. For the Sanctuary, only the best was fitting.

And, I must say, no handsomer pair of worshippers ever entered the doors of the Tabernacle. I see them yet, the giant of a man, exuding strength and power, and the woman with the face of a saint, from whose brooding eyes welled forth a world of tenderness and love. There was no hypocrisy about it and no superstition. It was very real. How real I did not know until I was a grown man. Then I learned a secret.

I had a sister called Lizzie, a beautiful, radiant girl with golden hair and blue eyes. She was my father's darling and, being rather touty [1] in her youth, my mother's constant care. How much they loved her may be judged by a phrase my father used when Lizzie was going away. He said with tremendous sincerity : " Mind, Lizzie, my lass, if ever ye need me, call, and I will come to you to the uttermost parts o' the earth."

Not until I was a man did I learn that Lizzie was not my sister. My mother had a baby boy as her first-born child. The baby lived for one day. The manager of the mill where my father worked, hearing of the death, approached my father, who was then twenty-eight years of age, and told him that there was a wee fatherless bairn born that day to a lassie in the village. Would my father take

[1] Difficult to rear.—ED.

MY FATHER AND MOTHER

her instead of the one who had died ? My father and mother talked it over. It seemed to them the Lord's will that they should be father and mother to the unwanted wean. And Lizzie came to be suckled and cared for and to become the very apple of their eye.

Eighteen months later I was born.

In all my life I never heard my mother say a harsh word and I never saw her angered. To her, my father's will was her will. It was not a case of weak submission to him. It was complete faith in his judgment. For her, life was perpetual sacrifice. She did not think of it as sacrifice. Those who do their duty, thinking it a sacrifice, are liable to become embittered. My mother never lost her sweetness. Her husband and her children were her portion. In them and through them she lived. She counted and took care of the scanty wages. She planned out the week's needs. We never wanted ; and there was always something for those less fortunate and always a shilling or two laid by for an emergency.

We talk much in Scotland of our fathers, and those men of a generation ago were great in their own way. But the women of Scotland, the mithers o' Scotland, douce and true, hodden-doon but never girnin', hard-wrocht yet aye ready to lend a haun to anither in need, they are miracles.

Perhaps, seeing the people of Parkhead through the kindly spectacles of years, I have drawn them with a Kailyard goodliness. It is not untrue. They were almost all good and kind and, behind a rough appearance and manner, were very gentle.

Even the boys who went wrong were generous, warm-hearted fellows who ruined themselves, but would not knowingly have hurt anyone else. But not all. There were some who might have been the models for *The House with the Green Shutters* or *Hatter's Castle*.

There was one real scoundrel. He seemed to tick at nothing. Sometimes he disappeared. He would come back worse than ever. The last time I saw him was at the corner of our road. I was standing with a few of our crowd, cracking away, as was our custom after the Templars' Meeting. Across the street were three of the crowd we had no truck with.

Suddenly we saw the notorious one, swinging down the street. He was an ugly sight, for he had a black eye that spread from eyebrow to cheek. When he saw the three, he swung up to them, laughing, and said :

" She's deid ! "

" Wha's deid ? " they asked.

" The wean," he answered. " I'll hae nae mair to pay."

Then he led them off to celebrate his release from the result of his folly.

There was also a family who were regarded with something akin to awe. There was nothing against their morals. They were not drinkers or swearers or vicious. Yet we looked askance at them. They were hard, hard and cruel, hard as quartz. One of them was murdered in the street by a big, wild Orangeman whom he had hammered and had followed still hammering him, until at last, driven to frenzy, the Orangeman turned and stabbed him, for doing which he received a sentence of fourteen days' imprisonment.

The family was quite unmoved. Great big men they were, whose only motto was " Get on." They got on. One of them died leaving £36,000 and not one friend.

" They wud sink one anither in a spoonfu' o' water," was my father's description of them.

My reason for mentioning these men is that they were so exceptional as to be noticeable. They were not the pattern of the people. If there had been many like them the people would not have survived, for they crushed all who seemed to hinder them. For a novelist to picture one of the type may be true to life, though more often he paints him blacker than any human being can be— and live. But to write as if the whole village was of that type is to write a lie. Some recent books by Scottish writers in which the Clyde workman and the Glasgow citizen are pictured are utterly and vulgarly false. To slander one's own folk is a miserable way of earning money.

CHAPTER III

The Boy

AT five years of age I was sent to school and was put into what was known as the 'penny class,' so called because the reading-book cost one penny. The classes went up to the 'fourpenny.' I liked school. I was slow at lessons which involved spelling or writing. To this day I write very slowly, forming each letter as I did on my slate in school. But at memory work I was excellent. I enjoyed history. Moreover, I could recite all the major bones in the human body, and I knew the Bible stories.

In my second year at school I was awarded a prize for Bible. That was the first and the most sensational prize I ever received. It was an event in my life. To my father and mother it was an augury. They were beside themselves with pride. To think that their son had won a prize! I am sure that they dreamed that day the dream of every Scottish parent. They saw their son, summoned by name, march up the hall to receive prizes for learning. They saw him in the University bending his head to be capped Master of Arts. They saw him in the Divinity Hall. Yes, they saw him in Geneva gown and white bands, wagging his pow in a pulpit. Oh, happy dreams, in which the boy of six becomes a man of twenty-six, the ideal man ! Of course, they did not speak their dreams. My father, when I returned with my prize, patted me on the head, saying : " Well done, my cullan, we'll win through yet."

But the dreams were there. That night I was

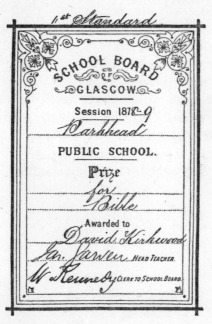

gravely escorted to the house of Mrs MacKenzie, known as " Auld Kenzie." It was not to see her that I was taken. It was to be seen by her son. This young man had come to Parkhead with his mother from Inveraray. His natural tongue was the Gaelic. He spoke English with that grammatical precision and clear enunciation which is common among the Gaels who have learnt English from the book. He was a lad o' pairts, who was working as a grocer's assistant and at the same time studying for the ministry, snatching spare moments from ham and groceries to study Hebrew and Greek. He was, except the minister, the most learned man in the district. What more natural, then, than that my father in his moment of exaltation should lead his prospectively learned son to see the scholar. To them I was " Wee Dauvit." As we entered, my father held forth the book which I had received, with the words : " D'ye see whit oor wee Dauvit's got ? " He opened the cover and read through from first word to last the label pasted on the fly-leaf, rolling out the words as if it had been a Royal Proclamation :

" SCHOOL BOARD OF GLASGOW

SESSION 1878–9

PARKHEAD PUBLIC SCHOOL

PRIZE

for

BIBLE

Awarded to

DAVID KIRKWOOD

JAMES GARVEN, *Head Teacher*
W. KENNEDY, *Clerk to School Board*"

Once more he held out the book to Mr Mac-Kenzie, as if to say : " Whit d'ye think o' that, noo ? "

Mr MacKenzie patted me on the head and said : " Splendid." Then in his Highland lilt, in which the *l*'s were as prominent as were the *r*'s in my father's speech, he read : " The Story of John Smeaton and the Eddystone Lighthouse." Turning over a page he read :

" This edifice is singularly remarkable as much on account of its height as of its massiveness. It is of exceeding usefulness, its fire burning night and day for the guidance of navigators."

It was pretty hefty stuff for a boy of six, but I devoured it, though I preferred the simpler and more stately English of *The Pilgrim's Progress*, a book of which I never grew weary.

That year of my life I remember also because of an incident that happened in the playground. The boys and girls were playing in the ' forenoon break ' when suddenly a boy of about twelve came running into the playground, stark naked. He seemed not to be going anywhere in particular, but ran round the playground like a dog with hysteria. The girls, who were probably well aware of the anatomy of the male, shrieked in terror. The boys chased the intruder. I stood still, full of wonder. Often I had bathed in the nude in the summer with a crowd of other boys. There was nothing unseemly about it. But to be nude in the playground was unseemly, and I was conscious of the boy's nakedness. I was dimly conscious also that there was a difference between a boy and a girl, that the difference was important, for the girls shrieked and ran away while the boys chased the laddie. In dreadful fear he ran out of the playground. Two things happened to me: first, I was aware of nakedness ; and, second, I recognized

in the epileptic what I had read about in the Bible
as a boy possessed of an evil spirit.

Childhood's impressions are graven deep and,
although forgotten, are not lost.

Never can I forget my first sight of the sea.   I
was eight years of age when my father and mother
took me for the annual trip of Brown's millworkers.   We sailed from Glasgow down the Clyde
to Garelochhead.   It was the first time I had ever
been in Glasgow, and it was my first view of the
wonderland of the sea.   I was frightened at the
quivering of the paddle-steamer.   As we sailed
down the river, I lost my fear in the fascination
exercised over me by the huge unfinished ships
lying on the stocks.   When the river broadened
and I saw water all around, I grew uneasy again.
How vast the sea seemed !   Then I caught sight
of the foaming water churned up by the paddles.
The sense of power drove out all fear and I learned
to love the sea.   It was no longer a barrier shutting
me in.   It was an avenue inviting me out.

CHAPTER IV

The House of Joy

EVERY man is the product of heredity and environment—and something else which science has not yet revealed to us. Heredity gave me a certain dourness and made me thrawn. Environment developed another phase of character.

The gladdest days of my life are associated with the Sabbath Morning Children's Meeting, which was held in a hall under the direction of " Mister Buchanan," surely the merriest saint who ever trod the earth. He was cashier in Templeton's famous carpet factory. That was his livelihood. But the morning meeting was his Life, and he shared it abundantly with us, a crowd of two hundred poor, bare footed, wee waifs, to every one of whom he was an intimate friend.

Mister Buchanan (for, in speaking of him, we always emphasized the ' Mister ') must have influenced thousands of lads and lassies in Park-head, for he carried on the meeting for thirty-seven years. To this day, when we foregather and talk of old times, we speak his name with reverence and love. He is the only man I have known who was never laughed at behind his back.

Mister Buchanan was a fine singer, with a

3

lilting rhythm that radiated happiness and joy. Before the doors opened, we were there, standing with our bare feet in our bonnets, to keep off the cold of the pavement. When the doors opened, we rushed in, like a burn in spate, to greet the warmth and brightness of the place and the man. There was no strict discipline in the meeting. It was not needed. We were all too glad to be there.

" Come away, children," called Mister Buchanan. " Come away, there's plenty of room ; and the closer, the warmer."

Then we sang our opening hymn, a hymn of happiness, for Mister Buchanan used to tell us that we should sing with a smile in our eyes. The result was that we were not stiff and solemn wee dummies standing to attention. We moved our heads and our bodies, laughing to each other as we sang :

> Best of the seven, O Holy Day,
> That sends a light o'er life's dark way,
> A day of praise and prayer.

Automatically we sat down and as automatically we bowed our heads as he prayed, finishing with the combined meeting repeating the Lord's Prayer.

After another hymn he told us a Bible story very simply, but dramatically. If it was about Joseph, we could see the camels of the desert. If it was Abraham, we could smell the faggots burning. After another singing, he would ask questions of the meeting : " Who was Joseph ? " " What was the name of his youngest brother ? " And so on, until we grew quite excited.

Sometimes strangers came to give an address.

We thought they were no good. Some of them were of the fire-and-brimstone order. We thought they were cruel. Mister Buchanan talked always in terms of love and kindness and happiness.

Every winter we had a party. "Buchanan's Soiree" was the event of the year. Children paid fourpence. Adults paid sevenpence. On entering we received a bag of pastries—three teabreads and a 'pastry.' With it we received an orange and a poke of sweeties.

Fighting for seats, we set up a howl: "Tea! Tea! Tea!" It was a real cry of hunger, for it was the convention not to begin eating until tea was served. The adults were affronted and called to us to be quiet.

"Did ye ever hear such a lot o' noisy weans?"

But Mister Buchanan enjoyed it, and would rattle his cup in his saucer, shouting: "Tea! Tea! Tea!"

Tea was a luxury and a great rarity. Occasionally on a Sunday my mother would give us a cup of tea. At "Buchanan's Soiree" we could have as much as we liked, and it was a boast among the boys that they had had three cups or even four cups. We drank many cups of tea, but most of the children kept some of the teabread to take home to their mothers. Then we had songs, sometimes a comic—always the favourite—and a juggler. Once I remember we saw a great mystery. A man with jars and wires made sparks and lit lamps where there was no gas. It was our first introduction to electric light.

On one ever-memorable evening, a sheet was

lowered from the ceiling. The gas jets were turned down, and we saw on the sheet coloured pictures of the life of Joseph. It was indeed a *magic* lantern to us. We were spellbound by the mysterious way in which the beautiful pictures appeared on the white sheet. After the first few, we cheered every new slide. We were in the age of novelties and were full of wonder.

For us there was no Christmas. Christmas had been abolished centuries before. It smacked of Anglicanism, the curse of Scotland, in the horrors of ' the killing times.' There was no New Year for us. We were too poor for presents or toys. A calendar from the grocer and an orange from the fruiterer were our only gains. But " Buchanan's Soiree " made up for everything.

So also in summer " Buchanan's Picnic " was our annual summer holiday. It was a great event, looked forward to for months. Did we not go in a train? Not very far, truly ; only to Uddingston, about eight miles off. But a train was an experience, and the country a fairyland. And the good things to eat and the races and the football made it the day of the year.

When I was old enough I joined a Bible class held in Black's Hall, a splendid place built for a public-house for which the owner never got a licence. The minister of Tollcross, a gey dull Hielan' man from Campbeltown, conducted the class. ' Conducted ' is the word. The contrast between " Mister Buchanan " and him was overpowering. The one was a laughing, splashing burn in the hills, the other was a puddle in a coal-pit. But in the first session I could have stomached a much duller man, for we studied *The Pilgrim's Progress*, my favourite book. He must have been good at his job as an expositor for, after the class, we spotted the characters in our own village from the studies the minister had given of them in *The Pilgrim's Progress*. During another session we studied the history of the Jews. It was heavy going, for there was no spark of imagination in the sodden peat of his mind. But the story stuck. Many years later I owed my life to the knowledge I had gained of the history of the Jews.

And, let me say it gratefully, it was this man who first loosened the bands that bound my tongue. " Like father, like son " does not apply to the Kirkwoods. My father was so ready in speech and so eloquent that I was overawed into silence. I often think that the reason why the sons of orators are seldom orators is, that they are afraid to begin, lest they fail by the standard set by their fathers.

I had no feeling for speech. My one ambition was to play an instrument of music. Pianos were few in the district and a fiddle was almost unknown. I never learnt to play. The next generation was not frustrated. Years afterwards, I noticed that one of my sons was a frequent visitor to the house of a neighbour. He had gone there for a message on one occasion and, seeing a piano, had sat down on the stool, fingered the keys, placed his hands on the keyboard and found he could play. Every other instrument came as naturally to his fingers or his mouth.

To return to my first trial of speaking. It was the custom for the two Bible classes ' conducted ' by the minister to have a " Joint Social " once a year. A social took the form of a tea-party, followed by a concert, and brought to an end with games. Some progressive spirit suggested that we should have a dance instead of games. As we deliberated on our programme, the minister and the chief elder were in the vestry. A youth named Andrew Gray and I were appointed as a delegation to the minister to submit the programme. At the end of the programme came the word " Dancing."

He looked at it with his solemn eyes and, in a voice like a moan of a sea-bird in a cave, said :

" And what will this be ? Is it dancing that is here ? You will not be allowed to have dancing here, to be sure."

I found my tongue.

" Do you no' believe in dancing ? " I asked.

" Indeed I do, but it is a pastime for the parlour or the drawing-room."

" But whit aboot us ? We've nae parlours or drawing-rooms," I replied with some warmth.

Instead of answering, he rose from his seat, left the vestry and went into the hall, where the young folk were waiting to hear the result of the negotiations of their delegates. He marched on to the platform and announced that he refused absolutely to allow dancing at the social.

My first attempt as a negotiator had been a dismal failure. It left me bubbling with hot indignation.

Andrew Gray later on became manager of Mount Vernon Steel Works, and I became his foreman. He is now General Manager of the Lanarkshire Steel Works.

I began this chapter with Mister Buchanan in my mind. I close it with this fact : A friend of mine, who has a wide experience of the theatre, has told me that he never thinks of Shylock but he sees Sir Henry Irving, and that he never thinks of Hamlet but he sees Sir Johnston Forbes-Robertson. Now, Mister Buchanan was a man of rather reddish hair and wore a moustache and beard of the kind which we associate with those men who have never shaved. So closely were his appearance and his temperament woven into my mind, that for years afterwards, whenever I thought of Jesus Christ, it was Mister Buchanan that I saw. And in all my life I have never known any man more worthy of the association.

Perhaps those who work in the unknown bypaths of life and see so little of the results of their devotion may be encouraged to hear that one who was of their number is so remembered after fifty years by a bare footed laddie who loved him.

CHAPTER V

The Age of Steel

WHEN I look back over the life that I have
lived, it is more like a dream than a
reality. A few years enable us to take a detached
view of ourselves and of the incidents which
seemed so world-shaking when they happened.
Distance lends disenchantment to the view. What
seemed catastrophes have become incidents. And
yet, there does appear as if there was some line
running through it all. It looks to me as if I was
born unto trouble, as the sparks fly upward. I
was not pitched head first into strife and trouble.
I had the temperament that leads a man where
trouble is. Whenever a man conceives a new idea,
or finds that an idea has taken on a new form, he
is on the way to becoming either a rebel or a
heretic. It is not an easy journey. Folk have not
yet emerged from the state in which they regard
new ideas as immoral and the men who hold them
as wicked.

There were many rebels in my young days.
We heard their names—Lincoln, Shaftesbury,
Simpson, Lister ; but they came as distant echoes.
The rebels we knew of more intimately were the
men who were changing the Age of Iron into the

Age of Steel. They changed our village into a forge and our weavers into the black squad. Just as the Age of Iron reached its zenith, Rigby invented the steam-hammer. In partnership with Kerr he laid down great iron-works in Parkhead. They brought from England a man, Beardmore, as the manager of the works. So was laid the foundation of the famous " Bairdmore's o' Parkheid." The great achievement of Rigby and Kerr was the steam-hammer " Achilles." Nothing like it had ever been seen in the world. It had a power of sixty tons !

The world stood aghast. But the brain of man is never satisfied. No sooner was " Achilles " at work than Rigby conceived a hammer of even greater power—nothing less than one hundred tons. At last " Samson " superseded " Achilles." " Samson " was the mightiest hammer ever created. " Achilles " defied the world. Some of the older folk in Parkhead thought that " Samson " was defying God Himself.

" It's no' canny," they said, " and nae guid will come o't."

It looked as if they were right, for when " Samson " let fall his hundred tons on the iron plates, the whole district quivered as in an earthquake. Dalrymple's distillery was shaken to its foundations and in the walls of " Rattray's Church " great gaps appeared. That was of little consequence to the creators of the giant. So delighted were they with the success of their new implement, that they entertained all the men in their employment to a social in the City Hall of Glasgow.

" Samson " was soon shorn of his glory, if not of his strength, by the birth of " Goliath." This monster had a six-hundred-ton fall, a prodigious power in those days. Once more " Rattray's Church " showed signs of cracking, though the firm had scarcely paid the charges for the repairs of the last shaking. Dalrymple's distillery began to rock.

Those who had regarded such gigantic creations as little short of blasphemy shook their heads wisely. They knew.

The hammers have gone. The distillery has gone. The church still stands. It is " Parkhead Parish Church " in the books of the history of Glasgow. To us it was " Rattray's Church," taking its name from its greatest preacher, as " Spurgeon's Tabernacle " takes its name from its great founder. The Reverend Alexander Rattray was a great preacher, very dramatic and compelling. The pulpit in Scotland, like the stage in all Great Britain, has forsaken drama and oratory. It is considered not quite proper to be earnest and enthusiastic, and rather vulgar to scale the purple patches of the mountains. Perhaps it is because they dwell only in pastures green that youth has grown weary of them. In the years of vigour we respond to vigour. The quiet waters are for the elderly.

Alexander Rattray was not afraid of purple patches. At his evening service, instead of speaking from a text, he took a subject of topical interest and sought to explain it against the background of spiritual principles. The young men and maidens flocked to hear him, and his addresses were the subject of discussion during the week.

I remember many of those evenings, but there is one which I remember as more deeply thrilling than any sermon, lecture, or play I have ever listened to. The subject was " Laurie and Rose." These were the names of the slayer and the victim of the Goatfell murder. Goatfell is the highest hill in the island of Arran, the finest holiday resort in the Clyde area. Rose, an English commercial traveller, holidaying on the island, had been seen in the company of Laurie, making for the path leading to Goatfell. Rose did not return and Laurie disappeared. The body of Rose was found on Goatfell with his skull smashed. Laurie was eventually caught, accused of the murder, but found to be insane.

On the evening when Mr Rattray preached on the subject of the murder, the church was packed. At each side of the pulpit reading-desk was a gas light. Before the sermon it was the custom to lower the lights in the church, but the two on the pulpit were left. On this occasion Rattray turned down the two lights. He described the walk of the men to the foot of the mountain and their ascent of its steep side. Then, as if standing on the peak, he surveyed and described the view, the river, the lochs, the islands, and the coast of Ayrshire. The effect was magical. We sat almost breathless. But the crisis was yet to come. Lowering the pitch of his voice without losing its tone, he described Rose, the stranger, standing, fascinated by the beauty of the scene ; and Laurie, creeping behind him, lifting a great piece of rock and crashing it down on his head.

As he spoke, he raised his hands slowly above his head, as if lifting a heavy boulder, and suddenly threw them forward at us with a huge throw. We all jumped as the imaginary lump of rock came crashing down upon us.

Unlike many dramatic speakers, Rattray was a stickler for truth. He hated exaggeration and inaccuracy. In order to give this address on the Sunday, he had travelled from Glasgow to Ardrossan, sailed over to the island of Arran and climbed Goatfell, so that he might note in detail the nature of the climb and the view by which Rose was entranced.

A few years ago one of my friends was going to open a sale of work in this church. I told him this story of the former minister, and he used it. To his surprise the women in the audience were restless and amused. After the ceremony two women told him the cause of the restlessness. They were the wives of two elders. They were known to all the people. Their names were Mrs Laurie and Mrs Rose, and they had been sitting side by side !

This sermon of Mr Rattray had a peculiar effect on me, apart from the moral of it.

The moral was that no man can foresee in what circumstances he may find himself, and, if we are to be able to withstand the blast of a sudden temptation, we must build our character firmly in our youth. The effect on me was to bring to my young mind the realization of the terrific power of speech.

From that day I understood, as never before, why my father and others spoke of Gladstone with awe. Although they had never heard Gladstone speak, they had talked with those who had ; and the spell was passed on from one mind to another.

It had a secondary effect on me, because I then understood how it was that the sayings of Jesus had been stored up by those who had seen Him.

But to return to the Age of Iron. The chief products of Parkhead Forge were tail-end shafts, crank shafts, stern frames, and keel bars. The keel bars were from fifteen to twenty feet long, four inches thick, and eighteen inches broad.

In the Age of Iron these bars had to be built up, layer by layer. A few hundredweights of scrap-iron were thrown into the furnace with the coal, and, when red-hot, were hammered on to the bar. Then more scrap, and another layer was hammered in. It was a long process and difficult.

But everything was difficult in those days. There was difficulty in making great forgings ; and there was difficulty in shifting them when they were made. I remember well how, when a tail-end shaft or a crank shaft was to be sent out, the whole shop stopped work.

The shaft was hoisted on to trolleys called a ' monkey,' and four or five hundred men, tugging great ropes, hauled it up to the top of the brae at Parkhead Cross, where horses were yoked to haul it down the Gallowgate.

To-day a motor-lorry will back into the yard, take a load twice the weight, and whisk it off without so much as a farewell wave of the hand. This is the Age of Petrol.

The revolution from iron to steel came with Murdoch's discovery of gas, and the putting down of the Coggan Mill, which could do as much work on a Saturday forenoon as " Goliath " could do in a month. There was no more heavy hammering, no more building up layer by layer. The revolution was upon us.

The Age of Steel had arrived, and machinery was displacing man.

And it found me with the ordinary preparation of an engineer. My home was a house of one room and kitchen on the top landing of a whitewashed building in Westmuir Street. We entered by an outside stair leading from the backyard, where was the water tap which had to serve the needs of twenty families. Our family consisted of father, mother, two sisters, and myself.

I left school when I was twelve years of age, just the usual poor wee boy setting out to make a living in a hard world, and wondering, as all wee boys do, what kind of a prize-packet the future held for me. I was not a weakling in either body or mind. I was small for my age, but as tough as a stirk. I had already resolved that life was a glorious thing. That had been the teaching of Mister Buchanan. But the fact was revealed to me when I was ten years of age, and made of me an incipient rebel.

To most of us knowledge comes slowly. Understanding comes in a flash. For me the process of knowledge has been slower and more laborious than for others. But it was in a flash that I first realized that life had death at the end.

A craneman in Parkhead Forge was burnt to death by steam. I heard my father and mother talk about it. The only impression their talk made on me was that the man had suffered pain. I did not realize what death meant.

There was a great crowd at the funeral, which was held at the meal hour. The men of Parkhead joined the procession at the gate of the forge. At the head of the procession marched a band. As they passed Westmuir Street, where I lived, all the boys stood and watched it.

The band was playing a hymn which I had sung hundreds of times. I knew it by heart:

> Childhood's years are passing o'er us ;
>   Soon our schooldays will be done ;
> Cares and sorrows lie before us,
>   Hidden dangers, snares unknown.

Although I had sung the hymn hundreds of times, the idea of it had never entered my head. I was ten years of age. Childhood seemed eternal. My schooldays looked like enduring without end. Every day was a day of joy, food and home, and games and fun with other boys.

Suddenly, as the band played the tune, my mind repeated the words. I was transfixed with horror. I was not to be a child much longer. School would soon be over. And then ? Cares and sorrows, dangers and snares.

How dreadful it must be to be grown up, with

happiness all over and no more laughter and fun !
And then death !

One day my mother would die and my big
strong father would die. I was horror-stricken.
My mind was so shaken that my knees shook in
sympathy. Then there came a thought of rebellion
against such a thing. Why should I have to grow
up and live with care and sorrow, I, a wee boy,
so happy and so content? It could not be true.

From that hour I have hated that tune and the
words of the hymn. I was taught that it was true.
It is not true. It is a sin to let children think it
is true. Children should set out in a brave new
world of high endeavour and radiant happiness,
for life is a glorious thing.

But when I hear that tune, I quiver with a
memory of the moment when I first understood
the meaning of the words.

CHAPTER VI

"*The Guiding Star*"

IT was the ambition of my father and mother that I should be a tradesman. They knew what it was to live on a labourer's wage of about eighteen shillings a week. The crafts were looked upon as the aristocracy of labour and, at that time, when engineering was beginning to become a great industry, the aim of most parents was to make their sons engineers.

I could not start as an engineer at twelve, and meanwhile I was in sore need of a pay. I had to find a job of some kind. My teacher at Buchanan's Sunday forenoon meeting, Robert Bolton, found me a situation as a message-boy in Murdoch's printing-works in Buchanan Street, Glasgow.

Bolton lived in Springfield Road, fully a mile from where I lived. I set out from the foot of Westmuir Street at seven o'clock in the morning for Springfield Road to meet him, and we walked together along the London Road to Buchanan Street every morning—a trudge of about three miles.

I worked till six o'clock at night, and then walked home again. All I had to eat was a 'piece' in my pocket. My wage was 3*s*. 6*d*. a

4   49

week. After a fortnight the Factory Inspector came on the scene, pronounced me to be too young, and Murdoch's were forced to dispense with my valuable services. I was one of the first victims of the social legislation of which I was later to demand more. On that occasion I heartily disapproved of it.

That was my first experience of being unemployed, and there was no dole. To the poor, experiences come early.

I ran about for nearly a fortnight, until I got a job as message-boy with Archibald Scott, grocer, on the west side of Bellgrove. It was a high-class shop, and I carried messages to Dennistoun.

On occasions, I had to take a two-wheel porter's barrow loaded with messages to Springburn, three miles away, and most of it uphill. It was agony. I was small for my age, and so lightly built that I was known among my friends as " Wee Davie." What awful struggles I had, straining every nerve and muscle to pull that two-wheel barrow up the steeps of John Knox Street, with the great walls of the prison on one side, the Cathedral and the Necropolis on the other, and in front of me the Royal Infirmary ! The solid masonry made me feel ' awfu' wee.'

As I passed these great buildings and went on uphill through Castle Street, Springburn seemed to be miles and miles away. I cannot remember any occasion when anybody gave me a hand up that hill with my barrow, though sometimes I have stopped in the middle of the hill, dead-beat and weeping. The world is kindlier nowadays.

Even if it were allowed to-day, I am certain that if any boy had to do that job, there would be about twenty men and lads who would run forward and give him a hand.

I stuck it for six months, because the four shillings a week was of vital importance. Then I heard that Watson's at Parkhead Cross required " a message-boy with experience." That was meant for me. I made personal application for the job.

The three days between my interview with George Watson and the coming of the news that I had received the job were as anxious a time as I experienced while waiting on the result of the 1918 election, when we had to wait a fortnight from the election day before the declaration of the poll, in order that the soldiers' votes might be recorded.

I was so glad to have the job that, when the Fair came round, I went to the shows where a man took photographs on tin. I paid sixpence to be taken. I had to cross my legs to hide a large patch in the knee o' ma breeks—an early example of the personal vanity of which I was to hear so much in later years.

My mother was so proud to have my picture that she forgave the extravagance. Real photographs were rather a novelty and quite the fashion. They were called ' *cartes de visite* ' by the photographers. We simply called them ' photies.'

Each works had a ' photie club,' into which the workers paid sixpence a week until enough was gathered to allow us " to hae oor photies ta'en."

I was with Watson's for two years, until I was

old enough to be apprenticed as an engineer. I started off at J. and T. Boyd's (Shettleston Iron Works) to serve my time as an engineer. I worked from 6 o'clock in the morning till 5.30 at night, and my wage was five shillings weekly.

At 8.30 we stopped for three-quarters of an hour for breakfast, and every morning I ran full pelt from the works to my home for my breakfast, a distance of about one mile and a half. Then I ran back, taking my dinner in my pocket. My dinner consisted of 'breid and jeely.' [1]

At 5.30 I came home for my supper—porridge and buttermilk, and sometimes bread and butter and a cup of tea. Our principal food was porridge and buttermilk. Only on Saturdays and Sundays did we have a hot meal, which usually consisted of broth, made with half a pound of boiling beef and a marrow-bone, and potatoes. We were very fond of broth.

At this time we were very poor. I know that now. Then it never entered my head, for we were never in want. Whatever my parents may have felt of our financial inferiority to others, I had no real sense of it. Indeed, on one occasion I had a distinct feeling of superiority.

I was about fourteen years of age. In Camlachie, a district about two miles from our house, was an encampment of gipsies and show-people. Every year, after their wanderings, they wintered on a large open space. On a Saturday night I was walking with my father, when a gipsy couple came out of a public-house with a boy at their

___
[1] Bread and jam.—Ed.

MYSELF, AGED THIRTEEN

side about my own age. The couple were drunk. They were quarrelling, shouting, and swearing. And the boy walked along beside them, whistling!

Of poverty and degradation he was unconscious. In what seemed to me misery, he was contented and happy. Whistling! It would have broken my heart.

I walked beside my father. For the first time I was conscious that I loved him and was glad that this man was my father. I knew we were poor. I knew that there was a difference between us and some folk who were called ' comfortable.' But it had never made me miserable or ashamed.

But I knew that if my father and mother had done what the gipsies were doing I should have been both miserable and ashamed. Besides, they looked so poor !

But the other boy was whistling !

I did not finish my apprenticeship with Boyd's. After three years I told my father that I could never become an engineer there, as they were machine-builders. My father agreed, and got me started in Duncan Stewart's, Bridgeton, where I almost finished my time.

Then two young men, David and James Tullis, who served their time with me, set out to start an engineering shop in Parkhead to build laundry machinery. Although I had not quite finished my time, I went with them and was their first outside man. I was with them until they removed to Clydebank two years later. The present owner, David Tullis, and I built the first engine for driving laundry machinery. I went to a laundry in Dumbarton and assembled it. It is running to this day, after forty years.

I had now reached twenty years of age. Young manhood was just beginning to dawn, and I began to grow in every way from the time I was eighteen till I was twenty-two.

I was still a very poor youth, living at the foot of Westmuir Street, but experiences were building up my mind and my body. What Mister Buchanan's forenoon meeting had meant to me in my childhood, the Good Templars meant to me in my youth.

I had joined the Juvenile Lodge of the Good Templars when I was a schoolboy. It was a ritualistic affair, founded, I understand, on the model of the Freemasons. I remember the ritual to this day, and at one of my trials in England, when I was invited by the Bench to say something in my natural tongue, I recited a swatch of it, to the consternation of the whole Court! On reaching sixteen, I was promoted to the Adult Lodge, the " Guiding Star." The company was good. Youths and maidens met together for ritual and for instruction and for amusement. We had a dance every Saturday night. On being promoted, I got in touch with three or four of a group called " The T.T. Youths," all older than myself. These lads worked in Boyd's, and were also members of the Good Templars.

I was proud of their friendship. Boys of sixteen are flattered by the friendship of men of twenty, and copy their habits. I am thankful I had Matthew MacLean, John Roy, and James

Hendry as my men friends. From that time on I became one of "The T.T. Youths" and active in the I.O.G.T.

At the age of nineteen, as a result of hearing a man speak in the open air, I bought Bellamy's *Looking Backwards*. I read it and re-read it, and, without knowing much about politics or economics, I began to think along the lines of Socialism. I could not understand it all, but I felt it was right.

I gave the book to one of my friends, John Roy. He was the son of an elder in the church. His father found him reading it, took it from him, and, lifting the 'rakin' coal,' put the book in the fire, and that was the end of my *Looking Backwards*.

The 'rakin' coal' was the equivalent in the home of damping down the fire in the works or smooring the fire in the Highlands. Working-men used to leave the house at five in the morning; consequently the fire was never allowed to go out, so that they could have a cup of tea and toast before starting.

At night, before going to bed, the lump of coal was put on to keep the fire going through the night. In the morning the lump was broken and the fire blazed up.

Although my father was not a Socialist, he had none of the hatred of Socialism which was common at that time, and for long afterwards I remember thinking, when I heard about my book, that my father was a better man than John Roy's.

I had read about Protestant books being burned, and I suppose that the hatred I had for the Church that did that became directed against the father of John Roy. It just shows how a young man's outlook is influenced by his early upbringing. I was growing up a Puritan Socialist.

At twenty years of age I began to notice that young men chose different ways of life. Side by side with " The T.T. Youths " there grew up a kind of club called " The Jolly Twelve." The story of these young men, whom I knew well, I have already told ; but as this record would not be complete without that story, I will set it down again.

The drink habit was very strong among artisans in those days, and youths were started off drinking with a sort of initiation ceremony. Among a certain set it was considered a manly thing to drink.

Every lad wants to get over the years of change as quickly as possible. He feels he ought to be a man, but he knows he is not. That makes him shy. Often fine young fellows drank in order to get rid of that shyness. For many it meant disaster.

It was in protest against this custom that " The T.T. Youths " was formed. It was to show their manliness—and I say that in its true meaning, not as a sneer—that " The Jolly Twelve " was formed.

We were all friends. We had been at the same school, and the only class distinction among boys is the distinction between a decent chap and a sneak. " The Jolly Twelve " were not sneaks. They were thoroughly decent fellows, good-natured and easy-going. Even the worst of them was kind-hearted, and every one was devoted to his mother.

The class distinction appeared later on and just before we left school. Then the boys of the middle class were better clad, had different manners, and were quicker at their lessons. Gradually the two classes drifted apart; not all of them, but most of them. The sons of the middle class tended to keep among themselves and to hive off from the sons of artisans and labourers. The sons of artisans and labourers had a similar inclination to keep apart from the sons of the middle class.

There was a difference in our fathers also, because the artisan and labourer had very little money, and no hope or means of increasing it. All that they earned was hardly enough to carry them through the week.

The middle class—shopkeepers, merchants, etc.— though not rich, were so much better off that they seemed rich. Their businesses could grow and make them richer. Consequently they thought of money, not for what they could buy so much as for what they could save to increase their businesses. They were hard and domineering men.

But our mothers were much alike, warm-hearted, gentle women, bound up in their children, especially their sons.

" The Jolly Twelve " set out to have a good time. So did we. We found ours in a Temperance Hall, where we met for lectures, concerts, socials, and the rest of it. We also went to night school. We had no money. " The Jolly Twelve " had money from their mothers. They had the evenings to themselves, went into Glasgow and came home late, often the worse for drink, when they would become noisy, swearing young men. They called it ' seeing life.'

By the time we were in our twenties there were stories going around about one or other of " The Jolly Twelve." Some were in trouble. Some lost their jobs and could not find new ones. Some did not look for jobs.

In due course our group settled down and married. Some of us had met our wives at the Club concerts and parties. By the time we were nearing thirty the line of life of the two groups began to tell.

This is what it told for eleven of " The Jolly Twelve." The other I lost sight of.

1. Son of a house-agent ; committed suicide by poison at thirty.
2. Son of a manager ; married at twenty-eight ; two years later found dead with throat cut.
3. Son of a merchant ; cut his throat in a stable at thirty-one.
4. His brother ; went very low ; accepted £250 for marrying a girl, and disappeared at twenty-five.
5. Son of a shopkeeper ; died in a lunatic asylum at thirty.
6. Son of a shopkeeper ; drowned himself in the Clyde at twenty-six.
7. Son of a shopkeeper ; poisoned himself at thirty-two.
8. Son of a merchant ; bairned a lassie and fled the country.
9. Son of a shopkeeper ; jumped from a bridge into the Clyde at thirty-five.
10. Son of a coal-merchant ; committed suicide at thirty-six.

11. Son of a warehouseman ; cut his throat in a Glasgow hotel at thirty-five.

The longest lived of the eleven died at the age of thirty-six.

Now I trace the line of life of the other group :

1. Became manager of one of Beardmore's mills, and died at sixty-three, leaving a fine family.
2. Went as a young man to U.S.A., sent back at age of fifty to superintend erection of vast works in England, of which he became manager; still living.
3. Became a joiner ; succeeded to his father's business, which he still controls.
4. Became a slater, and subsequently a partner in the business, which he still controls.
5. Became engineer and works manager ; retired well-off.
6. Started as butcher's message-boy, and now owns business.
7. Apprenticed to builder ; now foreman in one of the largest firms.
8. For forty years has held a high position in leather factory.
9. Apprentice, wright, and now master-builder in Glasgow.
10. Clerk, and now manager of large business in Glasgow.
11. Myself.

Of the eleven of " The Jolly Twelve " none lived beyond thirty-six, and eight killed themselves. I know of none that left children, but one committed suicide a week before his son was born.

Of the eleven of the other group, all are living except one (who died at sixty-three). Every one prospered, and their families prosper also.

CHAPTER VII

The Journeyman

AT the age of twenty I joined the Amalgamated Society of Engineers. My father thought I could not be considered a complete engineer until I was a member of the Society. I joined the Parkhead Branch because the Secretary, Thomas Hargreaves, was a leading light and a 'guiding star' in the Good Templars.

I had had some experience beyond the usual by this time. The year before, I had been sent to Dublin to erect the boiler engine and machinery of a new laundry—the first steam-laundry in Ireland. To me, going to Ireland was like going to a foreign land. I knew many Irish in Glasgow. It would be untrue to say that we were one people. Religion and race, perhaps religion more than race, kept us apart. But we knew each other well enough to understand each other. It was quite another matter for me to go to Dublin, right into the midst of a foreign people. My head was full of stories of the Fenians ; and the murder of Lord Frederick Cavendish in Phœnix Park was still very much alive in our minds.

Still, " where duty calls or danger, be never wanting there." I went. I found the builders still at work on the building. The leading man, a big, swanky, red-haired Irishman, had not spoken ten sentences to me before he told me he was a Fenian. A Fenian! Oh, horror! I determined I would not let him see I was scared.

"An' whit's a Fenian, onyway?" I asked.

I had to repeat the question. It was a light to a lamp. He glowed. For twenty minutes he thoroughly enjoyed himself telling me of the aspirations of his people. "All for Ireland," he kept repeating. I am certain he used the words "Sinn Fein," pronounced "Shin Fane," but some of my friends tell me Sinn Fein was of later creation. That big fellow had a "Shin Fane" of his own. Perhaps he created the phrase. He hated the English. He pictured them as cruel and greedy snobs, tyrants of the deepest dye, the despoilers of his land, the oppressors of his people. The "Scotch" were not quite so bad, but the difference in their grade of iniquity was so trifling as to be imperceptible.

"An' whit are ye goin' to dae wi' me noo I'm here?" I asked.

He was quite surprised at the question. Do to me? He was going to treat me as a friend and a guest of his country. I was to understand that this hatred was not directed against me or any other individual. It was not "the Englishman" or "the Scotchman" they hated. It was "the English" and "the Scotch," and his idea of them was unlike any individual I had ever met.

We became the best of friends, so close that I

knew that he had something on his mind. His love of Ireland was almost a religion with him. He was ready to sacrifice all for Ireland. His love of his land was as intense as his hatred of England. I was conscious that such a contrast, pure white against pure black, would lead to trouble. A few days later the Four Courts were burnt down. I often have wondered if he lived to see the Rebellion of 1916 and, in his old age, the establishment of the Irish Free State.

During all the weeks I was in Dublin I met this strange paradox : a terrible hatred of England and a kindly friendliness towards me. I was surprised also to find that so many English and Scots lived in Dublin, apparently in very happy circumstances and without molestation. It was the England of the Viceregal Castle and Lodge they hated. The individual they treated with hospitality and goodwill. I confess that at that time I had no very high opinion of the governing classes myself !

On leaving Tullis's, I spent eighteen months at Binnie's Nail Work and Rolling Mill before reaching my ambition by being started in Parkhead Forge.

I had been in Parkhead Forge for two years when a strike broke out for an eight hours' day. The London engineers had struck for this, and also for the right to say who was to man the new machines which were revolutionizing the industry.

This strike was important. It was the first beginning in the engineering industry of the question of dilution of labour and the eight-hour day. The engineers all over Britain had by this time formed a Union, and were supporting the London men.

The employers on the Clyde decided that, unless the Clyde engineers stopped supporting the London men, they would lock out 25 per cent. of the men in their shops every week until they were all locked out. They put up notices to that effect in the Clyde district. I saw them myself.

Parkhead was not affected because Beardmore's was not in the Federation. To these notices the engineers of the Clydeside replied by downing tools so that the employers would not get the chance of locking them out 25 per cent. at a time. Parkhead engineers were working when all the others were unemployed.

A week or two later, while the Clyde men were still out, I happened to go into the old turning-shop in Parkhead to grind up my chisels, and my attention was drawn to the fact that they had put on two labourers, " Hammer Broon " and " Wee Bobby the Slinger," to work crank-boring machines. " Hammer Broon " was a very popular fellow. He played full-back for the Parkhead Junior Football Club. " Wee Bobby the Slinger " was also very popular because of his great skill as a slinger.

I said nothing at the time, but went to Richard Nisbet, who was Chairman of our Branch. He was an outstanding figure in the Forge on account of his ability as an engineer. He was also one of the very few Socialists in Parkhead.

He went to the old turning-shop to see. When he reported what was happening, the Works were seething with excitement. No one objected to

" Hammer Broon " or " Wee Bobby " themselves, but we knew that they were doing engineers' work at labourers' pay, and, if that was allowed, our pay would come down to the labourers' level and then the level of the labourers' pay would be lowered.

Richard Nisbet called a meeting for that night in Parkhead Public Hall. When we assembled, he proposed that I should take the chair. I refused. I had never spoken in public, and was by nature very shy.

Nisbet took the chair. Sandy Hornell moved that we demand that the two labourers be taken off the machine at once, or we would go on strike. A delegation was appointed to approach the management. The management refused point-blank to recognize the Union or negotiate with the men.

A strike was therefore declared. It was incomplete. Many men of long service and long membership who came out the first day went back to work the next, and others began to drift back. Those who were for staying out were in a fix. Some began to doubt the wisdom of it. Others feared the aftermath. I had to face my own position. My father was dead. I was the sole support of my mother and my grandmother. One of my sisters paid her way. She worked in a mill. The other was learning to be a dressmaker. It was my 33s. 4d. a week that kept the household going.

One of the oldest men in the Forge came to my mother and begged her to persuade me for my own sake to move that the strike be called off.

He told her I was a marked man, and, unless I did something to end the strike, I should not be reinstated.

My mother knew what that meant. She gave me the message. There was a sort of hope in her voice that perhaps I would agree. But I saw fine that she was not pressing.

" But ye will dae whit ye think richt," she said.

In a flash I understood that, in her eyes, I was no longer a laddie, but a man. I told her I would not move a finger to call off the strike.

A few days later the drift back to the Forge was more pronounced, and a meeting was called for the purpose of discussing the position. I knew that I was regarded as a prominent man. I was only twenty-three, but my opinion was often asked during the strike by men much older than myself, and even the leading men like Richard Nisbet treated me on a basis of equality.

It would be just sham if I pretended that I was heedless of it. I appreciated it. All the same, it was largely accident that made me prominent. There was a man in the Forge, a turner by trade, who was almost fanatically against the strike and against the Trade Union. He was a good workman, but very dressy and vain.

We used to refer to him as " a mighty man " and say with a wink : " He is going to be a foreman." He made a boast that, while every other man might need a Union to protect him, he needed no protection.

He could make his own way in the world, he said, and would stretch himself up, a big, deep-chested young man. He liked to parade his knowledge. One day, when we were talking about Scotland and England, I quoted Sir Walter Scott's lines :

> Breathes there the man with soul so dead
> Who never to himself hath said,
> This is my own, my native land !

He wafted me to one side with a wave of his hand and said : "Ye needna be quotin' Shakespeare to me. I hae read him as weel as you !"

Somehow he got it into his head that I was responsible for the strike, which was absurd. But he blamed me, and, after seeing me picketing at the works gate, trying to persuade men to come out and join the strike, he looked upon me as a dangerous man.

He bought a revolver. He not only threatened to shoot me, but told others that he was going to do it. A queer thing for a man armed with a revolver to call me a danger and to think of doing murder because of my ideas !

It is often the way that an idea is regarded as dangerous and a revolver as a protection. As if you could shoot an idea !

I mention this incident because it was one of many cases in my life where those who disagreed with me helped to make me important. It was this turner with his revolver who first negatively acknowledged me as a leader of men. It was partly his talk about me as a leader that made men accept me as a leader.

At the meeting to discuss the strike situation

it was resolved to take a ballot vote : " Continue the strike " or " Return to work." I was appointed one of the tellers. The other was a planer nick-named " the Whale."

We retired to count the papers.

The vote was for abandoning the strike.

When the time came to announce the result, I found myself alone. " The Whale " was nowhere to be seen. He had left the hall.

I announced the result of the ballot, and we decided to present ourselves in a body to our foreman on the following morning. When we reached the Forge, " the Whale " was already back at his job.

My foreman was James Kerr, the only Trade Unionist among the foremen. We, millwrights, could not go to him because he had been sacked on account of his connexion with the Union. So we interviewed the acting manager, " Wee Stocks."

" Wee Stocks " was from Jamaica. He was a very religious man. He had a whole string of pious phrases which he delighted to roll off his tongue. We came up in a body. We told him we had come back to work. Then, looking the picture of piety, he said :

" You, Anderson and Johnston, in accordance with our arrangement last Wednesday "—that was two days before the meeting—" will start work on Monday. But as for you, Nisbet and Kirkwood, you have made yourselves too conspicuous, and William Beardmore says you are not to be allowed inside the gates. Moreover, nobody will get started unless he agrees to leave the Union."

We were dumbfounded. Would the men accept work on such terms as the abandonment of the Trade Union, and without an effort to obtain the reinstatement of James Kerr, Richard Nisbet, and me ?

They accepted. In those days the fear of losing a job was a terrible thing. Unemployment meant starvation.

Nisbet and I were heartbroken. He had risked all for the cause of the men. He had lost all ; for the incident shook his faith in their will to " haud thegither." The incident did not affect me in that way. I was very young and believed that the men had the will to " haud thegither," but dared not face the consequences.

But it shook my faith in the honour of men who were known as being very religious. One of them had burnt my book, *Looking Backwards*, and now another had bargained with men in secret to break their loyalty to their fellows.

Well, " the Whale," Anderson, and Johnston were back at the Forge. Nisbet and I were out.

" You will never be allowed to show face in Parkhead Forge again ! " I was told ; but ' never ' is a long time, and you never can tell.

James Kerr, the foreman, who had been sacked, was not physically strong, so the men in Parkhead clubbed together and helped him to open a barber's shop. There was a wonderful feeling of comradeship in those days.

Some months later, on a Saturday morning, I came out of Kerr's shop, shaved and smart. I was standing talking to five labourers of Parkhead

Forge when I noticed them beginning to laugh. I looked round, and there, coming across the road, was the hero of the revolver, the man who had boasted that he would shoot me.

He wore a Lord Dunraven cap—very much the rage among the middle class—a double-breasted reefer jacket, and shepherd-tartan checked trousers. This was his attempt at a yachting rig-out, appropriate to the excitement over the *America's* Cup Race between *Vigilant* and *Valkyrie*.

He was reading a Glasgow newspaper, looking very important. He saw us with the tail of his eye, but, instead of stepping aside, walked straight up to me and said : "What are ye looking at ?" I said : "I'm sure I don't know."

Then he called me by a foul name. Without thought, my right fist shot out, caught him under the chin, lifted him off his feet, and he crashed on the back of his head on the stones of the road.

In the moment in which I felt my fist against his face I knew I had done wrong. When he crashed like a log on the road, I thought I had killed him, and there and then I vowed I would never hit a man again. But in less than a minute the yachtsman was on his feet, dizzy but uninjured.

Then followed an amusing scene. Raising his index-finger he pointed first to one man and then to another, and said : "You seen Davie dae that ?" To which he received the same reply from each : "Seen him dae whit ? Whit wis it he did tae ye ?"

Exasperated, he picked up his cap and went away.

Many years afterwards, that turner applied for admission to the Society. The Branch brought up against him the revolver and the threats, and were for refusing him. I thought that was foolish. I proposed that he be admitted. It was agreed, and the Branch never had a more loyal member.

A few years later, when I had some influence in the Crane Work, I was instrumental in having him reinstated when he had been suspended through lack of work.

Nisbet and I remained unemployed until the strike on the Clyde was ended. His rage was terrible. It seemed as if all his hopes were blasted. One day when he was very angry, I imitated my father and quoted :

> Ye'll find mankind an unco squad,
> And muckle they may grieve ye.

It made Nisbet laugh and say : " Man, Davie, Burns kent a' aboot it."

After that he became more reconciled. At last the Clyde strike ended, and the Clyde workshops were opened.

The men had lost. Nisbet and I, being marked men, had no hope of a job in Glasgow. We set off together for Clydebank, twelve miles away. We had with us Andra Lockhart, small of stature, but a rare wee soul. We started out without much hope in our hearts, but at Camlachie we had a bit of fun.

Standing on the pavement as we passed was Mickey McKeown, the famous Celtic international back. Just as we came alongside of him, Mickey

McKeown came up to Dick Nisbet and said : " Hello, Hislop, how are you getting on ? Come on and stand us a drink." Nothing would persuade McKeown that Dick Nisbet was not Hislop of the Rangers, a famous forward.

This cheered us on our way, and at last we reached Clydebank. All along Clydeside we had passed shipyards and engineering shops. They were busy, but full up. No one needed me, David Kirkwood, engineer, late of Beardmore's, Parkhead. No one needed Dick Nisbet, and as for Wee Andra, he seemed a pathetic wee creature, so footsore and weary with his long tramp. This was my first entry into the district. Ultimately we reached J. and G. Thomson's, now the great shipyard called " John Brown's," the cradle of great ships. It was our last chance. Clydebank was the boundary limit of the industrial area. Beyond that lay road and river, woodland and pasture, to Dumbarton Rock and the bonnie banks o' Loch Lomond. Squaring our shoulders, we marched up like the Three Musketeers, Wee Andra betwixt Nisbet and me, both nearing six feet. We asked for the foreman. He came. His name was Jake MacDonald. I'll never forget him.

" Ony chance o' a stairt ? I'm a fitter," I said.

He looked at Nisbet and me and said : " Come back the morn an' I'll see if I can fix ye. Jist gang stracht intil the yaird."

Then he looked at Andra. He pursed his lips and shook his head. No hope for Wee Andra.

When we were alone, Andra said : " Whit'll I dae ? "

Nisbet squared his shoulders and said : " Ye'll jist come doon wi' us the morn, Andra, an' we'll a' gang in thegither."

Next morning the Three Musketeers were at John Brown's. We marched " stracht intil the yaird " and lined up at the box where the engaged men gave in their names.

" Richard Nisbet," said Dick.

" Right," said the clerk.

" Andrew Lockhart."

" Right."

" David Kirkwood."

" Right."

We were a' ta'en on !

Not long ago, as I stood on the platform among the guests of the firm and watched the great Cunarder *Queen Mary* glide into the river, I thought of a weary, disillusioned out-o'-work seeking a job, and hoped that I had repaid part of my debt to John Brown's.

We were started on H.M.S. *Europa*. Then we were on H.M.S. *Ariadne*, and after that we wrought together on the first battleship built for the Government of Japan.

It was a terribly long day. We rose at 4.30 A.M., caught the 4.57 train from Parkhead to Clydebank, and reached home about 7.30 at night.

I worked in John Brown's for eight months. By that time I was a done man. I asked Jake MacDonald to give me my lying time. He refused, so I walked out of the yard and took a train from Clydebank to Glasgow Green Station. There was a little engineering shop run by Glen & Ross just at Glasgow Green Station. I went in and asked for a job, and was started right away.

Two or three days later I discovered that they did not pay what the Union had decided should be the standard rate of wages. I told the foreman that I would not break the standard rate, and he said he would try and give it to me, though they could not pay it to the other fitters.

I refused the preference and left. He said I was a " thrawn deevil."

I did not tell them at home that I was out of a job, as I knew it would upset my mother and grandmother ; so next morning, with a 'piece' in my pocket, I walked down past the gate of Glen & Ross and on to Glasgow Green, where I lay down and ate my breakfast.

I then walked to Inglis's Engine Shop at Whitehall Street, Anderston, and waited till the men came out at breakfast-time. The last man to leave the shop was John Methven, the foreman. I did not know him, but had often heard of him. He had the reputation of being a driver, but a man of upright and honourable character.

At that time Inglis's had the reputation of putting out the finest engines on the Clyde, and prided themselves on their fine craftsmanship. Methven would have nothing but the best. If there was the slightest fault, he would scrap the job. He supervised every detail personally.

Once, in the course of conversation, I referred to the leading hand. He flared up. " The leadin' haun ? Who is the leadin' haun here ? There's only wan leadin' haun here and that's me."

When Methven came out of the works, I asked him for a job. He grumphed and passed by. I waited until he came back from breakfast. He was the last man in. Again I asked him for a job. He looked at me and said : " Hae ye ever worked in a marine shop ? " I said : " No, I have not. I cam' oot o' Parkhead Forge, but I wis in J. and G. Thomson's, though no' on marine engines."

He asked me a lot of questions about my experience, and then said : " Weel, come in and we'll see whit ye can dae, but min' ye, yer on trial." I remained with Methven for three happy years until Inglis's was burned down.

Richard Nisbet had by this time become foreman at the new Steel Works, Mount Vernon. Reading in the newspaper that Inglis's had been burned down, he came to my home expecting I was oot o' a job, and offered to take me on at Mount Vernon Steel Works. This was one of the kindest acts that I had yet experienced. Richard Nisbet was a great engineer and a most lovable man, big in every way.

I started at Mount Vernon. In three years I became engineer foreman. Being a foreman, I felt I was in a position to marry, even though I did have to support my mother and grandmother. Young men were not afraid of undertaking responsibilities.

It had taken me a long time to reach the position. In the Good Templars it was noticed that, when lads and lassies became about eighteen or nineteen, they seemed to pair off. I found myself drifting naturally to the side of one of two sisters who were members. Just as naturally, another youth, William Harvie, seemed to drift towards the other. We became a quartette. There was this difference between Harvie and me. I was plain and rugged. He was good-looking and perfectly proportioned. He was a great footballer. He played against England and Ireland as a Junior. As a Senior he played for Clyde and Derby County. He was always an amateur. All the girls were soft on Harvie, but he preferred Grace Smith. One day, when he was twenty-three, he came to me and said : " Whit d'ye think o' this, David ? Grace says she'll no' gang wi' me unless I give up the fitba'. She says I've to choose between fitba' and her. Whit'll I dae ? "

" I canna help ye in that," I said. " Ye maun settle it yersel."

" But she says it wud be a disgrace to mairry a fitballer, and says I'll no' get her unless I gae to the evening classes an' read books."

" Weel, it'll mebbe dae ye mair guid than fitba'."

He renounced football and married Grace. She was an independent lassie. Her mother had died when Grace was an infant, and she and her sister were brought up by a grandmother who had had eight sons and three daughters, all of whom did well. Yet she herself seldom went farther from the house than the back court. Her children became artisans or married artisans. Her grandchildren entered the Civil Service or professions and now hold positions of importance in Britain and America—a not unusual story among the people of Scotland.

I was in Rothesay on my honeymoon when I was sent for by the manager of the works, Andrew Gray, my colleague of the " Joint Social." I returned at once. His first words to me were : " Dick's away, and I want you to come and run the show."

I said I was sorry, but that I was not going to take Dick's job. He grinned, and said I had better wait till it was offered to me.

" Weel," I said, " we're great frien's an' I won't take his job."

Gray then said : " Dick is not coming back ; that's definite."

I went to see Dick, and he said : " I have burned my boats. I am not going back. Take the job. I'm delighted to know you will follow in my footsteps."

I went back, accepted the job, and began the first week of my married life with a rise of ten shillings, which was like a fortune.

I was not twenty-seven. For three years I remained at Mount Vernon, and then, owing to an unfortunate difference with the manager, I left. I went straight to D. Y. Stewart's at St Rollox.

They were strange men in Stewart's, the roughest crowd of labourers in Glasgow. They appeared rough to me. How they would have appeared to an outsider, I do not know. To the outsider, Glasgow men and Glasgow manners appear abrupt and rough and uncouth at all times. Even in their friendly chaff, they seem as if at any moment they would exchange fun for fists. It is a convention to appear crude, to

adopt a sort of ' plain fact and no nonsense'
attitude.

But should anyone adopt a similar attitude or
imitate their mannerisms, they resented it and
showed their resentment. I remember an occasion
when a young man, who was rising in the Trade
Union world, and, later, proved to be one of the
best Trade Union officials I ever knew, came to
address the workers at Stewart's, as a prospective
municipal candidate.

He came from Falkirk. Having heard that the
men were a rough, swearing crowd, he thought
that the right way to approach them was to use
their own workshop language. He began with the
ungrammatical tongue, common among us.

" Ach, he's nae guid," a man muttered behind
me. " He's nae eddication."

After a few sentences, the candidate began to
use swear-words. Immediately there was an
uproar.

" Awa' wi' him ! " shouted the men. " We're
no' here to be insulted."

He could not go on. The meeting ended.

" Whit wey did ye no' gie him a hearin' ? "
asked one man of another who was notorious for
his roughness. He flared round and shouted :

" I'm dam' shair he'll no' come here wi' his
sweerin' an' blasphemin'. He should think shame
o' himsel'."

My job was a filthy one, and I had much less
pay than I had before. I stuck it for six years,
as black as soot the whole time.

That workshop was riddled with sectarian controversy. The workers were mostly Irish. Orange and Green formed two camps, and often their rivalry developed into a stand-up fight. They were called " Billy and Dan," from King William and Daniel O'Connell.

I did not know what to do, but at last I made up my mind to beard the lion in his den and go to Parkhead Forge and ask for a job. I went to see Mr McEwan, the head repairs engineer, in the machine shops. He paid one farthing an hour more than anybody else for fitters, but was considered the severest and the justest foreman in the works. McEwan started me as a fitter.

The ' never ' of Wee Stocks had not lasted long ! I was back in the place where I belonged— Beardmore's o' Parkheid.

The first job I had was the laying down of the machines of what eventually became the great Arsenal at Parkhead. This was in the year 1910. We laid down the most accurate machines for the purpose of making big guns.

For a whole year they produced nothing. The shops lay empty. I had the job of testing the machines and levelling up the shears of the lathes which were to turn and bore out the guns. It was beautiful machinery, working to a thousandth part of an inch. It was the finest gun-shop in the world. Guns and armour-plate are in perpetual rivalry. The gunmaker sets his mind and hand to produce a gun which will pierce any known armour-plate. Immediately afterwards, the chemist is called in to make a new armour-plate strong enough to resist the shell from the new gun. From the year 1900 this process had been going on, and in great arsenals like Woolwich, where the machines had been made for a six-inch bore, new bits had been added to the machines, as the bore of guns was extended to 8 inches, to 10 inches, and to 12 inches. Their machinery, therefore, though useful, was a patchwork affair. Other gun-shops had begun with small-bore guns and later adapted their machinery to suit the change to larger bore. In Parkhead we started off with machines that would build guns with a 16-inch bore.

I have often thought it a very peculiar thing that in Parkhead, where, from 1910 to 1914, there were about a thousand men at work, no one ever whispered that there might be some special reason why such elaborate machinery was being laid down, although there were no orders for guns.

In 1914 the place began to hum, and by May it was in full swing. During that month there was a ceremonial visit paid by a large delegation of Germans from Krupps's Works in Essen, who went over the whole of Beardmore's works, and were particularly interested in the elaborate machinery for making heavy guns, some of them even taking notes in their pocket-books! So much for our " secret preparations " for war with Germany !

In June 1914 King George, Queen Mary, and Princess Mary paid a ceremonial visit to the works. They were given a great welcome. Parkhead, though very democratic, was very loyal. After the visit, the gun-shop was quiet again.

There was no demand for heavy guns. Our men were paid off. I was retained, but, as there was nothing to do, I asked for a transfer to the Crane Work, where I started as a fitter.

No one thought in terms of war, but in less than a month the world was in flames.

CHAPTER VIII

War !

THE outbreak of war found Beardmore's men
physically and mechanically prepared, but
mentally unprepared. Within a week, the so-
called " international solidarity of labour " was
exploded by the force of national patriotism. All
our resolutions, fraternal greetings, and " inter-
nationals " faded into thin air. With few excep-
tions, our Socialist comrades abroad threw the
whole weight of their influence into the war scales.
At home the Labour Party, the Social Democratic
Party, and the Trade Union leaders did the same.
Only the Socialist Labour Party and the Independent Labour Party held aloof.

I had been bred in the idea that Scotland was
the greatest country in the world. I had seldom
been out of Scotland, and had been to very few
places in Scotland apart from Glasgow and the
Firth of Clyde. The history of Scotland I knew.
The geography of Scotland was a closed book to
me. But Scotland was the very breath of my
nostrils. Scotsmen were to me the finest race of
men. The engineers of Scotland were the finest
engineers. The songs of Scotland were the sweetest
of all songs. The religion of Scotland was the

6

only true religion. I could roll off stanzas of the order of : " Oh, Scotia, my dear, my native soil ! "

I revelled in the story of Scotland's struggle for liberty. I saw her battered but never beaten, rising from the crushed ashes of her blasted hopes to higher resolve and fuller power. I felt my body tingle as I sang *The Battle o' Stirling Brig* or *The March of the Cameron Men*.

Yet I hated war. I believed that the peoples of the world hated war, and had no hate for each other. A terrific struggle tore my breast. I could not hate the Germans. They loved their land as I loved mine. To them, their traditions and their history, their religion and their songs were what mine were to me. Yet I was working in an arsenal, making guns and shells for one purpose—to kill men in order to keep them from killing men. What a confusion ! What was I to do? I was not a conscientious objector. I was a political objector. I believed that finance and commercial rivalry had led to war.

I resolved that my skill as an engineer must be devoted to my country. I was too proud of the battles of the past to stand aside and see Scotland conquered. Only those who remember 1914 can understand the struggle of mind and the conflict of loyalties which so many of us experienced.

For some years before the outbreak of war I had been a Socialist, but I had taken no part in any movement except the Trade Union and Temperance. There were great discussions at that time about the Social Democratic Federation, which was in turmoil. H. M. Hyndman and

Harry Quelch, two of the foremost pioneers of Socialism, were being opposed by a younger school led by Yates, Matheson, and Tom Clark. When this group failed in their effort to capture the Social Democratic Federation, they formed the Socialist Labour Party. This Party had one outstanding feature. It was purely educative, setting out to pervade the people with the idea that in Socialism lay their only hope of economic progress. They used to tell the people not to vote for them unless they were in favour of Socialism. At that time there was a great deal of talk among the working class that certain individuals took an interest in the working-class movement only for the fleshpots of Egypt—that is to say, to become well-paid Trade Union officials. To prove that they were not of this type, the S.L.P. made it a condition of membership not to take a paid position in the Trade Union movement and to work for the cause and not for filthy lucre.

I joined the S.L.P. I was not a speaker. I had never addressed a public meeting, but I was active in the Trade Union Branch meetings, and always went to hear the great propagandists, such as Harry Quelch, H. M. Hyndman, Daniel de Leon, James Keir Hardie, and J. Bruce Glazier.

More important to me, I had met a man who was to exercise a great influence over me and whose friendship and loyalty I shall ever cherish. In 1909 I was asked by a friend to go with him to a meeting at which a Socialist candidate for the Parish Council, John Wheatley, was likely to be attacked by the crowd.

John Wheatley was one of the multitude of men of Southern Ireland who, having been brought over to the West of Scotland by their parents, have grown up in an atmosphere of divided loyalties. They love Scotland, but retain a deep affection for Ireland. They live in a very Protestant community and remain devoted and sometimes aggressive Roman Catholics. Educated at schools inferior to the schools of the Local Authority, they are below the standard of their Scottish neighbours, but have a quick wit and a marked fondness for public affairs. They seldom fall foul of the Glasgow folk, but are frequently in trouble with their fellow-Irishmen of the Loyal Order of Orangemen. Much of their antagonism is traditional and not personal. It finds a safety-valve in cheering their pet football team, the Celtic, many of whose players are Protestant, and booing their pet aversion, the Rangers Football Team, some of whose players are Roman Catholic. The converse is also true.

As a result of the ingenuity of youthful Pressmen, the Billy and Dan scraps which seldom do more than disturb the quietness of a noisy street, are described as " Riots in the City of Glasgow " !

John Wheatley was born in Ireland and brought over to a mining district near Parkhead in infancy. There he was reared in a house of one apartment. Having a strong leaning towards learning, he studied in his spare time. He was a coal-miner. He left the pits and became an assistant in the shop of a licensed grocer. He then worked for some years as a canvasser for advertisements for a local paper called an "organ of Roman Catholicism." At length he set up in business for himself as an advertiser. The business was unusual. Having obtained from the clergy the right to publish a New Year Blotting-pad, he gave them a few pages for parochial news and filled up many pages with advertisements of local tradesmen. The blotters were given free to the parishioners. It was a clever device and proved highly profitable. In time he became rich.

When I first met him, he was in trouble. He had declared himself a Socialist and founded the Catholic Socialist Society. This was too much for his co-religionists and their spiritual leaders. There was little they could do. They decided to do the little. They could not burn the heretic, so they made an effigy of him, which they carried through the streets and burnt amid much pious rejoicing at John Wheatley's front gate. He had been warned of the danger of being in the house, for an Irishman under the influence of religious mania, like one under the influence of alcoholic drink, is reckless. To the consternation of the inquisitors, John Wheatley stood with his wife at his open door, smiling at the fanaticism as if it had been fun.

The following Sunday morning he appeared at Mass as usual, and the trouble died down.

Now he was a Socialist candidate for the Parish Council, one of the humblest and most useful phases of public service. The rumour ran that the fanatics were going to give him a rough time. Some of us resolved to attend the meeting, ready to hand out fair exchange for anything that was coming. Nothing came. The meeting was orderly and attentive.

I had never heard a speaker state the case for Socialism with such simplicity and power. I recognized in him a true leader of men. We became friendly, and began the habit, which we maintained for years, of walking together in the country on Saturday afternoons.

John Wheatley was not much of a Party man. He had no association with the official machinery of the Labour Party. He was a member of the I.L.P., but at that time he was not regarded as of much importance. He had none of the oratory which was characteristic of most of the I.L.P. leaders. He was plain-spoken, direct, and simple. But he was gathering around him a number of men in the eastern districts who had been persuaded by his arguments to become Socialists. He was their leader and their friend.

In September 1914 I was still a member of the Socialist Labour Party. At a meeting of the Glasgow Branch a discussion took place as to our attitude towards the War. I moved that as a Branch we should declare our opposition to the War, and start an agitation for the purpose of stopping it. An amendment was moved that we support the War. The mover was John W. Muir, then editor of our paper, *The Socialist*, a quiet, thoughtful man of fine character and much respected. My motion was carried. Muir resigned his position as editor, and was succeeded by John S. Clarke, of whom I was to see much later on.

Recognized as a stop-the-War man, I was per-

suaded by John Wheatley to leave the S.L.P. and
join the I.L.P. He argued that, if Socialism was
to have any power, all Socialists must go into the
Labour Party and permeate it with the stop-the-
War ideas.

It was at this time that I came into personal
contact with James Ramsay MacDonald. With
John Wheatley, Thomas Johnston, and other
invited guests I attended a meeting in the Grand
Hotel to found a Glasgow Branch of the Union of
Democratic Control.

Ramsay MacDonald fascinated me. His head
was a thing of beauty. Black hair waved and
rolled over a fine brow, one curl almost touching
his straight, strong eyebrows, from under which
his eyes glowed. His voice was rugged, but soft,
and, as he spoke, there came into it a throb. It
was the natural instrument of an orator. Standing
upright, he was a splendid figure of a man, and
his appearance of height and strength was increased
by his habit of rising on his toes and throwing
back his head. He was the first man of culture
I had met.

That night John Wheatley and I became
Ramsay MacDonald's men, a fact which had
much to do with the thought of both of us and,
indirectly, a good deal of influence on the career
of Ramsay MacDonald. But that is another story.
At that time I was more of a Trade Unionist
than a politician. I thought more of Parkhead
than of Parliament.

In Parkhead I had become Chairman of the
Shop Stewards. The Amalgamated Society of

Engineers, the Machinemen's Union, the Union of Steam-engine Makers and Tool-workers were all at daggers drawn. I made it my business to lead them to act together, irrespective of their Unions. I had organized all the engineers in the Forge before William Beardmore knew I was back at the works. It was the best-organized works in Britain. We had no strikes, but by bargaining we secured unique concessions for the men and had persuaded the management to declare that none but Trade Unionists would be employed in the works—a rule which holds to this day and is adhered to in the letter and the spirit. When William Beardmore discovered that I was in the works and responsible for organizing the engineers, he wanted to have me put out, but by this time I was very popular with the workmen, and it was represented to him by the managers that the new system was much better than the old. The consequence was that, instead of being hostile either to the Union or to me, he began to be friendly. The friendship was soon put to a severe test.

In April 1914 I had moved in the Parkhead Branch of the Amalgamated Society of Engineers that we make a demand for twopence an hour increase. The wages were then 38s. 3d., and the increase would have made them 47s. 7d. This proposal was condemned by the Chairman of the Amalgamated Society of Engineers, Mr J. T. Brownlie, who called it ridiculous, stating that an engineer's rise was a farthing an hour, not twopence. The movement spread among the Clyde engineers, but still Headquarters intimated that a farthing was the maximum. The demand for twopence made me prominent down the Clyde. I was definitely opposed to enforcing our demand by a strike. I asked for a meeting between the employers and the Union. We were progressing fairly well when the War intervened. In November 1914 the question was raised again, but at a conference held in York our demand was turned down by the employers.

The Clyde men did not accept that decision. Our wages were lower than those of other trades- men, and we felt we were scabbing on every trade in the district. We re-opened negotiations with the employers, but made little progress. Then towards the end of the year—December 1914— J. & G. Weir's of Cathcart brought over a squad of American engineers. They were paid the rate we had asked for our own men, with a bonus of 17s. 6d. as well.

As a result of the inequality between the British engineer and the American engineer, Weir's engineers declared a strike. The Americans joined them, as they did not wish to be preferred. By this time prices for necessaries had risen so much that sixpence an hour would have been more reasonable than twopence an hour. In January 1915 the whole of the Clyde district engineers left work. We thought that our demand was so reasonable that, if we struck work, the whole of public opinion would be in our favour and that our request for a rise would be granted almost at once. We thought that the people would resent American engineers being paid twenty-six shillings more than the British engineers when we knew perfectly well that, though the Americans did their best, they were not nearly so highly skilled as our men. In this estimate of public opinion we were entirely wrong. Even our own Trade Union turned against us. The London Executive of the Amalgamated Society of Engineers came down to Glasgow and ordered us back to work.

I was by this time recognized as the head of the strike, though I had wrought hard to prevent it. I had passed from being a reticent Trade Union worker into being a leader. It was not a pleasant position. The public looked upon me as a pro-German and a traitor. They said I was holding back the supply of ships and munitions for which the Navy and the Army were in desperate need. They said I was consumed with vanity. They even called me a murderer, and said I should be put against a wall and shot. The passionate patriotism of that time was associated with hatred of Germans, and the hatred became directed against me. The Trade Union officials, who were ardent pro-War, called me disloyal. Every hand seemed to be against me. The Clyde engineers alone knew how I had sought peace. And they knew that the Americans were but the forerunners in a process which might wipe out the Union altogether. The question had to be settled now. Were the newcomers to work in the trade and as members of the Union, or were they to be regarded as men apart, to be paid more or paid less than the wage for which engineers had struggled for a generation?

I was Chairman of the Parkhead Shop Stewards.

The Clyde Shop Stewards asked me to state the case before the London Executive at a meeting in St Mungo's Hall. At that meeting I challenged Mr J. T. Brownlie with his statement that our demand was ridiculous when he was supposed to be advocating our case. Mr Brownlie's reply was : " I am a Caledonian like yourself and understand a joke." That was not enough for me. I was in no mood for jokes.

As the meeting proceeded, Mr Brownlie intimated that the Executive demanded that we should return to work. I moved that we should not go back to work until our just demands were granted. This was carried by an overwhelming majority, and we remained out.

Two days later I was invited to a discussion in the Central Hotel by Isaac Mitchell, an official of the Board of Trade, who suggested that we should accept one penny an hour rise. I agreed at once, and immediately summoned a meeting of the men at Parkhead, which I addressed. They agreed ; McManus, who was then in Weir's, agreed also. Meetings were held in all the works of the Clyde. The agreement was adopted. We all returned to work and, let it be said to the credit of masters and men, there was no victimization and no antagonism. Relations between me, as the Chairman of the Shop Stewards, and William Beardmore were resumed on a harmonious basis.

In recognition of my services during that exciting period the Glasgow Eastern Engineers presented gold watches to me and my wife.

This strike made a great difference to my

position in the works. I had the confidence of
the men and the management and from time to
time was brought into consultation with both
sides. Not only so, but the atmosphere of the
works was now friendly, and the result was a
greatly increased output.

It was shortly after the end of the strike that
I had my first interview with Sir William Beardmore. Although dilution of labour as a system
had not been begun, large numbers of outsiders
were being introduced into the works. They were
not Trade Unionists, and the wages they received
were less than the wages paid to Parkhead engineers. This created a bitter antagonism, which
often took the form of leaving the machines in
such a condition that the stranger coming on to
the machine would be delayed some time. Tools
were hidden. With a member of the Union, not
only would everything have been left spick-and-
span, but a man would often stay late to explain
things if necessary. The feeling in the works
became so bad that Sir William Beardmore asked
for a deputation of the shop stewards to meet him
to discuss the situation. I was appointed leader
of the deputation.

Sir William did not receive us in his room, but
in a bare side-room, where we stood in a half-circle,
as if we were looking for a job. While we were
waiting, the thought came into my head : " We
make our living out of Beardmore, and Beardmore
makes his living out of us. Why should he treat
us as inferior beings though he makes his money
out of us, while we are to treat him as a superior

LORD INVERNAIRN (SIR WILLIAM BEARDMORE, BART.)

being because we make our money out of him ? "
Just while I was thinking along those lines, the
door opened and Sir William appeared with a
manager, Mr Chisholm. Without a word of
greeting, he said :

"What's all this I hear about your Trade
Unionists in the work? I am going to have none
of this Trade Union here. I want to know if it
is true that the engineers are hindering the
strangers and making it difficult for them to
produce munitions because they are not in the
Union."

After some more of this, he said :

" I will have nothing to do with your Trade
Union. I have wiped my boots on the face of
the Engineers' Society twice, and I will do it
again."

The effect of his speech upon me was the effect
created on a little boy when being chided by his
schoolmaster. He had treated us as if we were
naughty boys. I was furious and let him have it.
I said :

" What you say, Sir William, is the truth. The
engineers are making it difficult for the strangers
to do the job. We have grown up with this work.
No one can do it as well as we can. It is a very
highly skilled industry. I know that the men are
hiding the tools, and I know that they are hindering
the strangers. I have never been placed in the
position myself, because of my job, but if I were
in the same position, I would do the very same
thing. If, coming into this Trade Union shop,
they will join the Union and work with the men,

every one will help them, but we will not help them so long as they remain out of the Union."

I told him that the majority of the strangers had joined the Union, and that no harm had come to them. We were now both very angry, and then a peculiar thing happened. Sir William was so staggered by the admissions I made, acting for the men, that he could not believe it. He turned to Mr Chisholm and said : " Chisholm, can this be true ? Is it really the case ? " To our amazement Chisholm said : " No, it is not the case." I turned to the delegation and asked them one by one if what I had said was true, and they all assented. Quite a change came over Sir William, and he said :

" Look here, Kirkwood, if anything like that happens in these works, you come and let me know. These are my works, and we have got to get on with the production of munitions. If I agree that none but Trade Union engineers are employed in these works, can I rely on you using your influence with the men in order to see that they do their part ? If there is any trouble, you will come to me. Don't you allow manager or anybody else to come between you and me. Let me know, and we'll sort it out. None but Trade Unionists will be employed in Parkhead from this time on," and he shouted : " Do you hear that, Chisholm ? "

Without waiting for a reply, and without saying another word, he marched out of the room.

This was a terrible experience. I knew that

what I had said to Sir William was an awful
revelation, and I knew that Chisholm denied it,
convinced that it was not true. I have no doubt
that Mr Chisholm knew nothing about it, and if
he had said he had not known about it, it would
have been different, but when he said it was not
true, I knew that it was a crisis, and that it was
either him or me for it.

We all liked Chisholm, and I must say in
testimony of his character that he never at any
time showed any ill-will toward me, but in our
almost daily dealings treated me as I treated him,
in the most friendly manner.

All the strangers joined the Amalgamated
Society of Engineers, with the exception of two,
and we decided to take no notice of them.

This happy state of affairs lasted for a few
months. I became a brick in the wall. I acted
upon Beardmore's request and went to him
repeatedly.

' Incidents ' were frequent.

Everything was being speeded up. New
machines were being packed into odd corners and
passages. New works were being created. Men
were working without any break on Saturdays or
Sundays, twelve hours daily, having to take their
meals at their machines or at the bench, and
allowed only twenty minutes to do it.

There was a tremendous demand for engineers
of all kinds, and the men began to realize that
they were important. The result was that there
was perpetual irritation. The foremen had no
control of the men, and the new manager, Admiral

Adair, knew a lot about ships, but had not the remotest knowledge of working-class life or Glasgow character. A finer man never came into the works, but he knew nothing about the men. He was most friendly with the workers, but his ideas of handling them were as foreign as if he had come from Mars.

It was in the midst of this seething mass of irritation, fatigue, excitement, and discontent that the Munitions Act was thrown like a bombshell. From my point of view, the most important effect was to show up how diverse were the outlooks of the officials of the A.S.E. and the workers in Parkhead. I found myself at complete variance with the officials. I was against the War. They were in favour of it. I was in favour of dilution. They were against it.

When the Munitions Act was passed, which forbade engineers from leaving the works where they were employed and seeking employment elsewhere, the officials of the Union came up to Glasgow to persuade us to support the Act, and called a meeting of the men. I was against the Act. I was appointed by the men to explain their position to the officials who had organized a great mass meeting in the City Hall, but the officials refused to allow any speeches to be made of an adverse nature. Mr Brownlie made a speech in favour of the Act. In reply, I called a meeting in Parkhead Works, and delivered the speech which I had prepared for the City Hall meeting. As this was the first big speech I had ever made, I took great pains with it. I still think it is about

the best speech I ever made. It came out of my
mouth like shells from a gun.

"Fellow-engineers, the country is at war.
The country must win. In order to win, we
must throw our whole soul into the production
of munitions. Now we come to the point of
difference. The Government and its supporters
think that to get the best out of us, they must take
away our liberty. So we are deprived of the chief
thing that distinguishes free men from slaves, the
right to leave a master when we wish to. If I
work in Beardmore's I am as much his property
as if he had branded a 'B' on my brow. . . .
They have us and they know it. Mr Lloyd George
claims that all this is necessary in order to win
the War. It is a strange doctrine. It amounts to
this, that slaves are better than free men. I deny
it. I maintain that for peace or war free men
are better than slaves. . . . We are willing, as
we have always been, to do our bit, but we object
to slavery."

As a result of this speech, things became pretty
hot for me, because many of the men were extremely
patriotic. On the other hand, there were a number
of individuals who were the very opposite. Some
of the most patriotic were my staunchest supporters.
Others thought that we should follow the advice
of the Union officials. Of the non-patriotic, most
looked upon a stoppage of work as a possible means
of bringing the War to an end. I wished devoutly
that the War might end. I wanted peace by
negotiation. I could not even think of peace as
a result of defeat. These two contending factors,

alongside of all the irritation caused by the constant working, made the atmosphere thunderous. The men were ready for anything at all. So was I. But little did I dream that I was to be swept into a hurricane.

CHAPTER IX

The Rebel

AS I have said, towards the end of 1915 the competition for the labour of engineers was intense. All kinds of people were starting new factories to make munitions who had never made them before. The factories needed engineers to teach the dilutees.

Many times I was asked to go to outside factories at a substantially increased wage.

Many things happened in those days which would be considered not only uneconomic but immoral to-day. The worker followed the politics of the employers ; he had only one thing to sell —his labour—and he considered it proper political economy to sell his labour to the highest bidder.

It was driven into our minds, not only by Trade Union leaders but by political economists, that this scramble was an unalterable political rule. Just as it was considered proper to withhold goods from the market to increase the price, so it was considered proper to withhold labour from the market to increase the wages.

Nothing could have been a temptation to me to leave Beardmore's. I belonged there.

Besides, I was in a unique position. I had the

confidence of the management and the men. I had the free run of the works. If a man got into trouble with his foreman, he would come to me and I would see the foreman. If a foreman got into trouble with his manager, he would come to me and I would see the manager.

If a manager got into trouble with the firm, he would come to me and I would go to see Sir William.

I suppose that no other man has held quite such a peculiar position in any great works as I had at the end of 1915.

Although I held this position of authority, I never had as much pay as a foreman, but, by every circumstance of my position as well as by my natural feeling, I was thirled to Beardmore's. I know of nothing that would have tempted me away from it. It was part of my life.

I was known throughout the Clyde area as " Davie Kirkwood of Beardmore's," and I was as proud of the association as was Sir William himself.

Sir William often chaffed me about the peculiar position I occupied, and on more than one occasion, when I was putting up a proposition to him, he said : " Look here, Kirkwood, are these your works or mine ? "

Another peculiar feature of my position was that I was in favour of dilution so long as it did not reduce the standard of life of the workers. I believed in the machine.

It was part of my philosophy to accept everything that would mitigate toil and give leisure.

Although I had had scanty education on the cultural side, I was a great believer in education, and for years before and after my marriage I went to night school.

I wanted more leisure for working people, but I wanted them to be built up to be able to use their leisure, for, as my father used to say, " Satan finds some mischief still for idle hands to do."

The outstanding feature of the Munitions Act was that it denied the men the right to sell their labour to the highest bidder.

This cut clean athwart the political economy of the hour, and to the men of Clydeside it appeared little short of slavery.

I felt it like that. I was happy in Beardmore's as a free man. I resented being in Beardmore's as a slave. I was part of the Forge by nature and by inclination. I would not be part of it by compulsion.

The Clyde's reply to the Munitions Act was the Clyde Workers' Committee, which had its representatives in every workshop. Meetings of protest were held, and the leaders met every Saturday afternoon to evolve new methods of self-protection against the Act and against the employers who, to us, seemed to be exploiting the patriotic sentiment that was abroad at the time.

The funny thing about it was that the members of the Committee were mostly men like myself, happy in their own special workshops. The strongest opponents of the Act were men occupying key positions in the works who, left to themselves, would never have dreamed of transferring their labour elsewhere.

I have always thought that this was peculiarly Scottish, to be struggling about the principle when none of us would have left the works we were in.

Some of the leaders in Weir's Works had never worked anywhere else, and would never have thought of working anywhere else. They were as much Weir's as I was Beardmore's. The same could be said of other works.

We attributed the Munitions Act to the quarrel between Asquith and Lloyd George. We knew nothing of the details. All we knew was that Asquith said there were plenty of munitions, and Lloyd George said there were not.

Mr Lloyd George became Minister of Munitions, and said he would go to the men direct. He arranged with Trade Union leaders to hold meetings in the large centres from London to Newcastle for the purpose of allaying in the minds of the men their suspicion of the Munitions Act.

The leaders of the Trade Union movement on the Clyde were in favour of the Act, and full of admiration for Lloyd George. We knew that they were backing him up.

The full-time officer of the engineers in the Clyde area was Mr Samuel Bunten, and of the boiler-makers, Mr Sharpe. These men went to Newcastle to welcome Lloyd George to Scotland and to arrange for a meeting in St Andrew's Hall, for which they had tickets printed.

A day or two afterwards they came back to Glasgow in a great rage. They reported that Mr

Lloyd George had refused their invitation to come to Glasgow.

They were so angry that they cancelled the meeting in St Andrew's Hall, and let it be known among the workers that the cancellation was due to the Clyde Workers' Committee, and that Mr Lloyd George did not want to meet the Clyde men.

Even the persuasion of Mr Arthur Henderson to the Trade Union officials was unavailing. They point-blank refused to carry on the meeting.

I was very much interested in this. I heard all about it in the head office of the Society from Mr Samuel Bunten. Bunten said that Lloyd George had said he would have nothing to do with us because of our carry-on, and was going to leave us to stew in our own juice. He gave me the impression that he sympathized with the attitude taken up by Lloyd George.

I resented this. There had been no carry-on.

Certainly the position was difficult, because the Trade Union officials were out of harmony with the men in the workshops. The Trade Union officials were death on the Clyde Workers' Committee, which they looked upon as usurping their rightful position.

Looking back, I am not surprised at their antagonism, because the Clyde Workers' Committee was perfectly organized and had a power in the Clyde area such as the Trade Union has never had before or since.

I returned to my work full of bitter feelings

against Mr Lloyd George for having insulted the men on the Clyde. The next day, while I was in the works, the gateman came to me with a telegram addressed to

DAVID KIRKWOOD,
PARKHEAD FORGE,
GLASGOW.

I remember still the twinkle in his eye when he said : "It's comin' tae it noo, Davie. We used to say 'Beardmore, Parkhead,' would find Sir William, but here it's you noo."

I opened the telegram and got a bit of a shock when I read :

LLOYD GEORGE WISHES MEET DAVID KIRKWOOD WITH SHOP STEWARDS AT PARKHEAD HEAD OFFICE THIS AFTERNOON.

At first I thought it was a trick, and I went with it to Jock Jordan, my closest companion and confidant, though ardently pro-War. He advised me to see Chisholm about it, and Chisholm said I had better see Sir William at once.

We went over together. Sir William was highly amused.

"You'll surely be satisfied now," he said. "This great man is coming to see you, not me. Do whatever is necessary to have every shop steward you can get. Make it a representative gathering. The offices are at your disposal."

When I came back after dinner, I found the entrance to the office blocked with a fleet of motor-cars and a battalion of police. I made to go in, but was stopped by the police.

I was not then so well known to the police as I became later on !

I had often heard of Mr Lloyd George's skill in stage-management. I have never known anything so badly managed as this meeting. Here were we, all on edge about the Munitions Act, but at the same time proud to meet the great Minister of Munitions.

We came to the meeting full of hope. It was bungled from the start. We knew Mr Lloyd George had arrived by the cars at the entrance. We arrived at the offices at the appointed hour, and were ushered into a large room without chairs or forms to sit on.

For forty-five minutes we stood together, waiting. After the first half-hour we were tired of each other. We were furious at being penned up. Some wanted us to go away.

I was not in the habit of being kept waiting for five minutes even by my employer. I was convinced that we were being kept in order to weary us.

I said to the men : "Look ye here, this is some of Lloyd George's doing. He's working some game on us, keeping us here, hopping off one foot on to another. Then they'll all come dancing in at that door, expecting us to march up and bow down. We'll stand where we are and let them come to us."

Some of the men made suggestions about letting them have it, but Jordan said : "Just leave it to Davie to haundle it. Naebody speak a word." That was a big risk, for I was by nature slow to take a bidding, and had become sullen with anger at the delay.

After three-quarters of an hour, what I had foreseen happened. The door was flung open and they marched in, all smiles—Chisholm, Beardmore, Adair, Lloyd George, Henderson, Murray of Elibank, and Weir of Cathcart.

The contrast was maddening. We were in our working clothes, weary and angry. They were fresh and prim, looking so challengingly well fed and pleased with themselves. At that moment I hated the whole crowd of them.

Just as I had said, they stood at their end of the room, waiting for us to march forward. Not a man moved. We glowered in silence. They smiled and chatted among themselves. They were of a different world.

Then, to break the awkward spell, Mr Chisholm came forward and said : " Kirkwood, why are you standing there ? Here's Mr Lloyd George come to see you. Come along up. You're making a fool of us all." Not a word of apology for being forty-five minutes late !

" No, no," I said. " Here's a fine cairry-on, keepin' us huddled here three-quarters o' an hour like a lot o' hens on a rainy day. Does he no' ken there's a war on ? We're here to produce munitions, no' to staun' idly by waitin' on him."

It is not necessary to tell me that this was crude and rude. It was highly disrespectful. But it was natural and spontaneous. I had no joy in it and no feeling of arrogance.

I was determined that the Welsh Wizard should not bamboozle us. To-day I am certain that it was the right thing to do. Those who are guilty of bad manners must expect a reproof, and to sit for forty-five minutes over cigars after lunch, while one's guests are standing waiting in another room, is bad manners whether for Cabinet Ministers or working artisans.

I feel like putting the next bit in ballad form :

> Then forth there cam' Lord Elibank,
> An' stracht and sure cam' he.

His face would thaw an iceberg. Fresh, calm, pleasant, and courteous, he was a new kind of man that had come among us. I have met many of his breed since then, these imperturbable gentlemen whom nothing can harass.

" Won't you introduce us ? " he said to the flurried Chisholm, as simply as if he was at a Co-operative Guild Social.

" Lord Murray, this is David Kirkwood."

" How do you do, Mr Kirkwood ? " said Lord Murray. " I am very glad to meet you. We have heard a lot about you. I am sure this is going to be a very profitable meeting."

By the time he had finished this sentence the others had come down to our end of the hall, and he introduced me to Mr Lloyd George. We shook hands. He held my hand and looked straight into my eyes.

" How do you do ? " he said.

" No' sae bad at a'," I answered.

He still held my hand ; then his eyes shone,

his face changed with a smile and he was radiant.
I felt he was trying to master me. He might
have done it. I don't know. He is a natural
hypnotist. The struggle ended by Lord Elibank,
as gracious as a queen, asking me to act as
chairman.

"I'm no' gaun to be chairman," I said.
"That canna be. I've been appointed to put
some pertinent questions to Mr Lloyd George."

"Oh, but that is quite right. You may put
all the questions you like. Act as chairman to
see the meeting properly conducted, and then use
your discretion."

I agreed, and was asked to introduce Mr Lloyd
George as "The Right Honourable David Lloyd
George, Chief Minister of Munitions for the British
Empire." I was in no mood for such a mouthful,
so I said :

"Fellow-workers, this is Mr Lloyd George.
He has come specially to speak to you, and I am
sure you will give him a patient and attentive
hearing."

Then I turned to Mr Lloyd George and continued : "These men are the Clyde shop stewards.
I assure you that every word you say will be
carefully weighed. We regard you with suspicion
because the Munitions Act with which your name
is associated has the taint of slavery about it, and
you will find that we, as Scotsmen, resent that.
If you desire to get the best out of us, you must
treat us with justice and respect. Now, Mr Lloyd
George."

He was flabbergasted. The radiance had left

his face. Instead of beginning a speech he asked me to question him.

" Oh," I said, " it's you that's come to deliver a message. You're no' satisfied with the production o' munitions. You want us to produce more."

That was the cue. He faced the men and started off with throbbing earnestness. Phrases came tumbling from his lips, " brothers in the trenches," " rain shells on the Germans," " insufficient labour." It was eloquent and persuasive, but it was all directed towards the dilution of labour, to which we were not opposed. Not a word about a share in the management of the dilution schemes nor about the workers being thirled to their employers' factories.

We therefore asked questions. He was a master at answering questions. But he would not deal with the " slavery clause." Then I used the two phrases which were remembered against me for many a day. I told Mr Lloyd George that the Munitions Act had bound the workers to Beardmore as completely as if it had branded ' B ' on their brows.

Many years later, in 1924, on the terrace of the House of Commons, Lloyd George was sitting with his family. As I passed, he called me over, introduced me to Mrs Lloyd George, Miss Megan, and others, and invited me to tea.

He took the table over, and told the story of this meeting in his own dramatic fashion, imitating my voice and gestures.

Then he told me what I did not remember,

that, as I used that last phrase, I had put my finger on my brow and made a capital 'B.' He said it sent a shiver down his spine.

When the story was over, he told us how Sir William had said afterwards : " That ' B ' on the brow business was absolutely ridiculous. David Kirkwood stalks about the works as if they were not mine but his. Slave? Dictator would be a better word."

How often it happens that our deadly seriousness of one day becomes the subject of humour the next, and that the contestants of to-day are the friends of the morrow ! They say in Parliament that the way to get on is to treat your friends as if they were going to be your enemies, and your enemies as if they were going to be your friends. But I wasn't built that way.

The other phrase which put me into boiling oil was the reference to Mr Arthur Henderson, dear old " Uncle Arthur," who looked upon all the engineers as his children.

Mr Lloyd George had said that he was not responsible for the Munitions Act, and that it had emanated from Mr Henderson and Mr Brownlie. That, in view of my talk with Mr Brownlie about cancelling the mass meeting, was a red rag to a bull. I turned to Henderson and said : " We repudiate this man. He is no leader of ours. Brownlie has been told the same to his face."

This was rank rebellion. It was not easily forgotten.

The meeting ended with good-byes all round. The great ones went away. We were left alone

ADDRESSING A MAY-DAY DEMONSTRATION AT GLASGOW

in the room. Suddenly I turned from the stewards, ran downstairs, and, as the motor-cars were about to leave, I asked Lloyd George if it was true that he had refused to have the big meeting with the men because of the Clyde Workers' Committee. He said it was absolutely false.

" Then will you have it ? " I asked.

He agreed to meet us in St Andrew's Hall on Christmas Day if I could organize the meeting, and on my telling him that the men would lose a day's pay coming to hear him, he said they would get their wages. I went back to the shop stewards, and we agreed to have the meeting.

What a meeting it was ! It was Christmas morning. The hall was packed. More than three thousand were in it. Hundreds were outside. Everything went wrong. Girl workers dressed in khaki were brought up from Georgetown and set on the platform. The Union Jack covered the table. A choir sang patriotic songs. Dozens of police were in the hall. Everything which the men regarded as ' kidding ' was there.

As Mr Lloyd George entered, the choir started *See the Conquering Hero Comes*. Then pandemonium broke loose. The audience started *The Red Flag*, which Bernard Shaw calls " the dismallest tune ever written." As Mr Lloyd George sat down, a lock of hair strayed over his brow. Shouts of " Get your hair cut ! " came from all quarters.

Uncle Arthur, as chairman, spoke in his most paternal manner, and far too long. We were all keyed up about the Munitions Act, but Uncle Arthur spoke about the neutrality of Belgium and the origins of the War. He had a bad time.

Mr Lloyd George began badly. He looked unwell, very tired. The audience was pitiless. As I was responsible for the meeting being held, I accepted a hint from Sam Bunten and, from the body of the hall, called on the men to give Mr Lloyd George a hearing.

They were quieter, and, seizing the chance, Lloyd George showed them what speaking could be like. He held them by describing quarrels about Trade Union conditions at such a time as " haggling with an earthquake."

Then he rolled off burning sentences about love of country and the awful struggles against the enemy. There was nothing of the problems which we were concerned about, and the row started again.

The meeting ended as a fiasco and made things worse instead of better. We were running hard downhill to disaster.

Next day newspapers had only an official report of the meeting. On New Year's Day *Forward* contained a full report. Before noon the offices were in the control of the military. Every available copy was impounded, the machines were dismantled and put out of action, and the paper was suppressed indefinitely.

That New Year's Day began the most exciting three months of my life. I felt that I was a marked man.

CHAPTER X

Storm

THE visit of Mr Lloyd George, looked at from the angle of the Clyde Workers' Committee, was a complete fiasco. Some of the more ardent members thought that it meant the end of the objectionable parts of the Munitions Act.

The most ardent are often the most optimistic.

I had no such thought. I had seen Lloyd George face to face. He was not the kind of man to be put off his stride by a rowdy meeting. I felt that his coming among us, working folk, was a master-stroke of an astute stage-manager.

It was the first time that a Cabinet Minister had come to the people informally, to talk to them man to man. He had taken a big risk to make peace with us, and we had given him a sword with which to smite us. I knew that he had captivated the country, including the Trade Unionists.

The only man of importance who had stood up against him was Robert Smillie, the miners' leader. The others were almost toppling over each other to lend him their aid.

They are now comfortably placed in Government positions. Lloyd George did not forget his friends. And they are doing their jobs very well.

We had made ourselves his enemies. I saw the country looking on us as irreconcilables, men who would accept no leadership and agree to no compromise. I knew that this was not the end, but the beginning of a struggle with an extremely able man who had the country at his back.

That night I had a good look at myself. I had won the complete confidence of the artisans of the Clyde area ; but against me were Lloyd George and his followers, the officials of my own and other Trade Unions, and a certain group of workers who were fascinated by the strange figure of John MacLean, M.A., a Communist, as sincere as sunlight and as passionate as a typhoon.

This group desired to stop the War at any cost, and would willingly have sabotaged the production of munitions to gain that end.

There I was, an ordinary workman drawing an ordinary workman's pay, but becoming the object of devotion and the target of abuse. That night I faced myself.

Of one thing I was certain—that I would not allow the Clyde, which had a reputation in the country as the centre of the most highly skilled craftsmen in the world, to become known as a nest of vipers.

Yet I was determined I would not yield on the centre point — the introduction of scab labour.

The trial soon came.

Lloyd George sent to Glasgow as Commissioners

three men of high repute—Mr Lynden Macassey, K.C., whom Sam Bunten described as understanding the whole position on account of having been trained as an engineer ; Mr Thomas Munro, Clerk of the Lanarkshire County Council, a man greatly admired for his courtesy, a dandy in dress and manner, and the possessor of an acute and agile brain in spite of smoking cigarettes end on end ; the third was my old friend, Isaac Mitchell, formerly Trade Union leader, and by this time promoted to the Board of Trade, where he still remains.

I was asked to call a meeting of the shop stewards at Parkhead to meet the three Commissioners.

That day the War news was terrible. Even reading of the awful slaughter made our gills white. We were all scared as the thundering masses of Germans tramped their way toward the coasts of Flanders. It was a subdued and saddened bunch of shop stewards that crossed over in their working clothes to Beardmore's office. There we met Lynden Macassey, Munro, Mitchell, Bunten, and Brodie, Beardmore, Adair, and Chisholm.

I hoped they would say : " Kirkwood, what can we and you and your men do to help the country ? "

Instead, we had a long speech from Lynden Macassey, with lurid word-pictures of the trenches, and the need for more munitions. He said there were machines without man - power and vices lying idle for want of fitters.

He ended by saying that all Trade Union

restrictions must go, and we must surrender our trade rights.

It was a great speech for a public hall, but there was no touch of intimacy about it. He was laying down the law. I was asked to reply, and I said :

" These trade rights are not ours to surrender. They are ours to defend. Our fathers fought for them. It is our duty to guard them.

" But we are not like the Luddites of old, who in their day and generation looked upon the machine as an enemy. We look upon it as a friend. As a Socialist I welcome dilution. But we will not allow the patriotic sentiment abroad at this moment to be a cloak under which to introduce low-paid labour and reduce us to the level of the textile-workers of Lancashire. That we will not have.

" But tell us your scheme, and so long as it does not degrade the workers we will help all we can. What is your scheme ? "

To our utter amazement they said they had no scheme ; they had not thought out a plan.

That seemed to me an insult, and I turned to Sir William Beardmore and said : " There you are, Sir William ! What's the use of sending men down here who don't know how to do their job ? Ye cudna rin a menage [1] that way, let alane a war."

Lynden Macassey stopped me. He glowered, his face tight-drawn with control. He said only one sentence :

---

[1] A club run by a woman who allows other women drapery goods to be paid for by weekly instalments.—ED.

" Mr Kirkwood, we do not know how it is to be done, but we are going to do it."

I was not such a fool as not to understand what that meant. I knew we must suggest the scheme. I took out a pencil and said :

" Look ye here. Here's a pencil. This pencil is a shell. You want shells to blow the Germans over the Rhine. This shell costs sixpence. Are you satisfied that that is the right price ? "

They all nodded.

" Are you satisfied to pay that price no matter who produces them—skilled, semi-skilled, or un-skilled ; male or female ? "

" Quite satisfied."

" Then we will do all in our power to meet your requirements. We will produce the guns, the shells, and all other munitions. In twenty-four hours we will submit a scheme that will satisfy both sides. We will give the production and keep the engineers safeguarded."

It was agreed. We had a friendly talk, and the Commissioners asked me to dine with them in the Central Hotel.

Sir William Beardmore, whose superb efficiency was tempered with a very human sentiment, gave a roar of laughter, and, putting his hand on my shoulder, said : " You needn't ask him to dine with you. He won't even take a cigar from me."

That night I went to John Wheatley. We collected shop stewards from other works. To-gether we thrashed out the problem, and John Wheatley began to write. In thirty minutes he had drafted the scheme. It was a perfect piece

of work. It has been said that John Wheatley
had not a creative mind. I disagree. But every
one must admit that his was one of the pre-eminent
constructive minds of his generation. It was like
a perfectly adjusted machine.

The next day we met the Commissioners.
With us were representatives of other works. I
read over the scheme and handed it to them.
They retired, leaving us to kick our heels, without
even a cup of tea.

One hour and a half later they trooped back.
They accepted the scheme without alteration.

It was John Wheatley who prepared the Dilution of Labour Scheme which became the basis for
the whole of Great Britain, and worked perfectly
until the end of the War.

Unfortunately, there were other elements at
work.

The out-and-out Trade Unionists attacked us
for having agreed to dilution. The extremists
attacked us for having agreed to increased production. John MacLean made me the theme of
innumerable speeches. These were disturbing.

But there were other troubles. *The Worker*, the
organ of the Clyde Workers' Committee, came out
with an article against those violent extremists who
proposed to use force to stop the War. It ridiculed
the idea.

The military people, who by this time had gone
daft, read the article as an incitement to the use of
force. My old friend, John W. Muir, the editor ;
Walter Bell, the printer ; and William Gallacher,
the President of the Committee, were arrested.

John Muir was charged with having written the article. He did not write it nor did either of the other two arrested men. The man who wrote the article was married and had a family of five children. John Muir was unmarried. He accepted the responsibility. There were only three persons who knew the author—John Wheatley, Rosslyn Mitchell, and myself. It was suggested that Muir should reveal the secret. He refused, saying :

" Some one is going to jail for this because the Military has read it the wrong way. If —— goes, there will be seven sufferers. If I go, there is only one, so I am going."

The trial was fought to the last word. But there had been found in the office of the paper copies of an Irish paper containing a foolish and flaming article by the Countess Markowitz. Great play was made of these papers. " You see what sort of literature this man harbours." The jury returned a verdict of Guilty. John Muir was sent to prison for twelve months, Gallacher for six, and Walter Bell for three.

Many years later John Muir was elected to Parliament and became Under-Secretary to the Ministry of Pensions. To the day of his death he never by word or suggestion went back on his word, nor did the others who knew his secret.

Another thing excited the people even more. House rents went soaring sky-high. The wives of soldiers did not have then the allowances of later years. They could not pay the increased rents. Thousands of men and women were pouring into Glasgow to work at munitions, and offering fabulous rents for houses.

Factors started to eject the wives of soldiers in order to let the houses to the newcomers who had money. The law-courts were crowded with eviction cases.

I found myself up to the ears in an organized campaign for resistance to the increased rents. John Wheatley, James Stewart, and Rosslyn Mitchell, all of whom subsequently sat with me in the House of Commons, carried out a platform campaign for the building of houses with money provided by the Common Good of the City and grants from the Government, free of interest.

That brought me trouble in the works, though I never stole a minute of my working day. I was called before Sir William. He told me he objected to me bringing him into " this housing business."

That remark touched my prophetic soul. I told him of the interest-free scheme, and was just warming up towards an oration on the subject when Mr Chisholm chipped in : " This is not David Kirkwood. This is John Wheatley and Rosslyn Mitchell. They are the men who are behind this crazy idea."

Sir William blew out his wonderful moustache and said : " I don't care who is behind it ; it's a dam' good scheme."

The " interest-free scheme " was a proposal that the Government should encourage Local Authorities to build houses by lending them money without interest, to be repaid in instalments over a period of forty years. The Government were to issue Treasury Notes to the Local Authorities as against the creation of the capital asset in the form of houses. It was a very simple idea, but was the object of intense opposition and ridicule.

When I saw that Sir William agreed with the proposal, I jumped at the opening. I knew that he had given a huge sum of money to finance Sir Ernest Shackleton's expedition to the South Pole.

Without any frills I said :

" Give me a quarter of a million, Sir William, and I'll cover these fields of Carntyne with houses. We will call it Beardmore Town. It will be your everlasting monument. You spent a fortune sending out men to seek unknown worlds in the frozen Antarctic. Do something for the world we know, here at our door. Beardmore Town, beside Parkhead, is a better monument than the Beardmore Barrier among the lifeless snows and ice of the Southern Pole."

He thought I'd gone crazy. My arms were stretched full length as I spoke. He looked at me, then lay back in his chair and roared with laughter. It was the most nonsensical idea he had heard. It was so far away.

To-day these empty fields, so far away, are dotted with cottages. The great Glasgow–Edinburgh arterial road pierces a new town of 10,000 inhabitants. It is called Carntyne. It ought to have been Beardmore Town.

" I have made Parkhead famous," he said to me one day. I agreed. But I wish he had made it beautiful. I know he was just the man to do it, if I had caught him the right way. This greatest captain of industry had a warm heart. He had

devoted his life to Parkhead Works. It was his
child. But it was ugly.

I must step aside for a moment to recall an
incident. One day one of the crack craftsmen in
the works made a mistake. He had a lathe for the
finishing cut of cranks, maybe just a thow—*i.e.*, one-
thousandth part of an inch.

On this occasion he under-cut it—that is, he
cut it under the size. That meant £1000 worth
wasted.

He went to the foreman in despair, a done man,
and asked to be let away. The foreman sought the
manager. The whole works was alert. The stage
was set for a storming row.

The manager sent for Sir William. Down he
came, smoking a cigar, as usual. He looked at the
crank—his lost £1000. Then he turned to the
manager.

" Can we make another ? "

" Yes, sir."

" Then get the thing done."

With that he walked away—a very god. " To
err is human, to forgive divine."

I must pull myself back to the strife and struggle
of the rent business. The M Shop in Parkhead
made howitzers. It was a new shop.

When it was seen that we were making little
headway with our rent agitation, the men in M
Shop passed a resolution that they would down
tools unless something was done in twenty-four
hours. I had nothing to do with this. It was a
spontaneous protest. The next day an eviction
case was to be tried. We knew it was a test case.

When the night-shift men finished their shift, they formed up in marching order. We marched to the Court, where we were joined by the men of Yarrow's, Henderson's, and M'Connell's. Thousands of us massed in the streets around the Court.

Meanwhile, John Wheatley and I sent a telegram to Lloyd George that unless the Government intervened to keep rents at pre-War level, the most important department in Parkhead would stop work.

This brought great trouble on my head. I was called to see Mr Chisholm. He was all dressed up, and horrified to hear of the threatened strike. " A strike," he said, " just on my one day off, when I am going to see my poor old mother."

Beardmore was in Inverness. We sought out Admiral Adair. He flamed up and blamed me.

" But I was in my bed," I said.

" I don't care if you were in Timbuctoo, you're responsible. Get a meeting of the men and I'll address them. There are no more patriotic men in Britain. Kirkwood, you will take the chair, but you are not to address the men. Leave that to me."

" Right you are," I said, and called the meeting.

He appeared like an admiral on the bridge of his flag-ship and gave a typical drum-head oration. The men were not impressed.

Then through the crowd a worker pushed his way, and with fiery eloquence he attacked house factors, the Government, and Admiral Adair. It was terrible, a torrent of blistering lava. The Admiral was shocked and grieved. He went away.

It took me two hours to persuade the men to return to work. One man, Sam Shields, refused. He went away home. That strike is always remembered as " the One-man Strike."

But every one could see that the human material was inflammable. Every day there were incidents, and though I was working at the bench, I was often called away. One day it was apprentices complaining that they were getting only ten shillings a week while their sisters were getting two pounds. I settled that. Next day it was the women workers complaining that, though it was the depth of winter, the workshop had no side-protections except tarpaulin and no sanitary conveniences of any kind. I reported to Sir William.

" Go along to the shop," he said. " Stop the work for a minute and tell the lassies everything will be put right." And it was.

Then came complaints about the appalling overcrowding in the workshops and the effect on the health of the workers through long continuous work at high pressure.

I advised Sir William to let the men have intervals for a smoke. He agreed. I went further and suggested that it would be a good thing to give the women a cup of tea. He arranged for tea to be served at 7.30 A.M., 11.30 A.M., and 4 P.M.

Everything was going sweetly. Without any vanity, I can say that both the management and the men had made me a pivot. I was the grievance hearer and healer. Whenever trouble started, I was on the spot to inquire and remove the cause.

Every department was open to me. Sometimes I went without asking permission. Sometimes I asked. It was never refused. The scheme worked perfectly.

Then, without warning, a bomb exploded under my feet.

First, I was refused entrance to one of the workshops, and, second, having been asked by the manager of the mill department to inquire into a stoppage of engineers at 5 P.M. instead of 6 P.M. on a Saturday, Mr Chisholm would not allow me to go to the mill department to inquire.

I was told that Sir William had given orders that I was not to be allowed to move about the works as I had always done. It was useless being chief shop steward, responsible for the swift settling of the many misunderstandings and disputes inevitable in a large workshop, unless I had the run of the place.

I therefore resigned my position as chief shop steward, and returned to my bench to operate the micrometer and the vernier in the business of gauge-making. But I interviewed Sir William, who confirmed the withdrawal of the privilege.

What fools they were ! They played direct into the hands of the M'Dougalls, the MacLeans, and their Russian friend, Peter Petroff, a queer figure who flitted about the Clyde area at that time.

I had had many a struggle with them in their efforts to stop work on the Clyde. I had been man-handled at meetings, called a fakir, a twister, and a traitor. The men of the Clyde knew I was fighting for them against two extremes.

When the management took away my privilege, which not once had I ever abused, they kicked away the prop upon which the men relied.

For a fortnight it was the talk of the works. Every effort was made to persuade the management to resume the former system. They refused. Then one night, on coming home late, I was told that the men of Parkhead had resolved to down tools next day at midday and leave the machines running unless I was reinstated in the position of freedom which, as Chairman of Shop Stewards, I had enjoyed.

Next day I went to my work as usual. At midday the works were empty. I left my bench, and, on reaching the yard gate, I found thousands of men, our own day-shift men, and all the night-shift workers from other yards on the Clyde. I was acclaimed as their leader, and, having made a speech, I said I would stand in with them.

That was on March 17, 1916. I had six more days to live as a free man.

In the afternoon the strikers met in the Louvre Picture-house. Thousands came. The streets were patrolled by policemen.

A great cheer welcomed me to the stage. It was a moment to turn a man's head. It might have turned mine had I not spotted in the dim light a group of soldiers in khaki. They had been sent home from France to work in the factory on account of their skill as engineers.

As soon as I saw them, I told them they must return to their work at once ; they were not free men. They were under Army discipline. If they were off work even a few hours they would be whipped off to the Army again.

Some of the shop stewards protested against my action. I would take no protests. The soldiers had to return to their work or I would return to mine. The soldiers reluctantly returned to work.

A few minutes later into the crowded hall marched Jock Dennistoun leading the electricians. Their shop steward came to the platform. As I saw them, I remembered having read that in Pittsburg, when electricians went on strike, a furnace had burst, the molten steel had poured into the mill shop and cooled, with the result that the steel floor had to be blown up with gelignite. I demanded that they go back to work lest anything dire should happen to the furnaces of the millworkers. They refused. The platform sided with them.

I stood and waited while the hall echoed shouts of " dictator," " tyrant," and " twister," and accusations of having " sold the pass " and " being bought."

What a battle that was ! The men who had cheered me in the morning were now cursing me as a traitor. The electricians refused to go back without the others.

We sent a deputation to Sir William. He sent them back. " Go back and get Kirkwood and I'll listen," he said, " but not otherwise."

The shop stewards and I went to the office. Sir William was deeply distressed, but would not restore the privileges I had enjoyed. We parted.

In the evening I had a promise from the electricians that they would go back at once. The others remained on strike, but they had by now realized that I had been right about the soldiers and the electricians. Indeed, the stand I took seemed to have as its reaction the effect of making me more of a leader than ever. For four days I moved about, the object of friendship to the men, but of execration to the public.

Women spat as my wife passed doing her shopping.

On the fifth day a man came up to me and whispered :

" Watch out ! If this affair is not settled, you are going to be arrested. I have inside information that they are going to hit hard."

I decided to make no move. But I did make one move. As treasurer of the Clyde Workers' Committee, I had at home a bag containing £200 in the new " Bradburys," one-pound Treasury notes. These I took over to John Wheatley and left in his care. Then I returned home and went to bed.

During the night Lloyd George struck.

CHAPTER XI

Hurricane

ON March 25, 1916, at three o'clock in the morning, I was sleeping the sleep of the just. I was awakened by a violent rat-tat-tat at the door.

My wife said : " That's them for ye noo."

The same thought flashed through my mind. I went to the door and asked who was there. A voice answered : " The police. Open the door."

" I will do nothing of the kind," I answered.

" You'd be better to open it. We have a warrant under the Defence of the Realm Act to take you to the Central Police Office. If you do not open the door, we shall batter it in."

I opened the door. There were four detectives with revolvers at their sides. I gave them the dressing-down of their lives.

" A fine lot of men you are ! Whom have you come to arrest ? There is nothing against me. I am not a savage or an anarchist. I never thought I would live to see the day that I would be taken away in this fashion. I have read of this kind of thing happening in Russia under the *régime* of the Tsar, but never dreamed that it would happen in Scotland to me.

" I never thought that Scotsmen would descend to take on a job to go and arrest another Scotsman who had done nothing, but simply was standing up for his rights and the rights of his fellows."

The police came into the house and said I had to come with them, and that they were doing all this under the Defence of the Realm Act, and were acting on the instructions of the " Competent Military Authorities."

I agreed to go, and remembering the experience of William Gallacher and John W. Muir in the police cells, I took two pairs of trousers to put on, because of the cold.

The police were very friendly, but they would not allow me out of their sight until I was safely lodged in the Central Police Office.

It was a novel situation for me. I had never been in the hands of the police in my life. I did not sleep all night. I had no blanket, and had just to lie on the floor of the cell.

About breakfast-time next morning I was brought out of my cell and taken before the Chief of Police, Andrew Stevenson, and Colonel Levita. I knew neither of them.

Colonel Levita read over the warrant and told me that I had been court-martialled the day before in Edinburgh and sentenced to deportation. I challenged him :

" How could I be court-martialled when I have never been at any kind of court in my life ? What does it all mean ? Where am I to go ? "

He said · " You can go to San Francisco or

anywhere you like, so long as it is outside of the Clyde Munition Area."

On the spur of the moment I said : " Well, I'll go to Edinburgh," and he said : " The very thing !—a garrison town." Then I gave him a bit of my mind.

" Why should you do this with me ? I have never done anything. You talk about the Germans. You are a Prussian yourself, to do this to me without giving me a trial. There is no evidence led, and I can produce plenty of witnesses.

" I have a character that will bear the closest scrutiny. There's nothing foreign about me. I am in the land of my nativity. You are a Prussian, that's what you are."

Levita said, " Take him away out of here," and I was taken back to the cell.

I was not aware of any others having been arrested. I thought I was alone. I remained in jail in solitary confinement. To me that was something terrible. Late in the afternoon two detectives came into my cell and said I had to go with them to my home to get some clothes, as they were going to put me on the train for Edinburgh, as arranged.

The detectives took me home in the tram-car. We got out at Parkhead Cross, and they walked one on either side of me.

Quite a number of the folk at Parkhead Cross recognized me, and followed us, so that by the time we got to the house there was a crowd of people.

By this time I knew from my wife that several

of my colleagues had been arrested. In the evening all the deportees were bundled into horse-cabs and driven to Queen Street Station. The detectives were above and below. Crowds had assembled outside the Central Police Office, and some of them clung on to the cabs.

In Queen Street Station I was handed a single ticket for Edinburgh and a ten-shilling note, and put inside the barrier. We were cast adrift.

We were told to report direct to the Chief Constable of Edinburgh, Captain Ross.

In the train were : Arthur MacManus, an Irish-man, afterwards made notorious as the alleged signatory of the Zinovieff letter and the British representative on the " Third International " in Moscow until his death ; James Haggarty, an Irish engineer, who, like MacManus, had originally been intended for the priesthood. I never under-stood why he should have been pounced on, for he had taken no prominent part in the trouble ; James Messer, one of the leading shop stewards in Weir's of Cathcart, a quiet, active, shrewd, and able man ; Sam Shields, a decent, hard-working, home-loving Bridgeton engineer, a typical fitter— he had for fourteen days been convener of shop stewards after I resigned ; Robert Wainwright, a young married man of high character and much respected as a workman and a man.

We were a subdued and anxious group. None of us knew what was to happen. I had left behind my wife with five boys and a girl. What was to become of them if anything serious happened to me ?

All sorts of ideas flitted through my mind. I knew I was regarded as the ringleader. They might shoot me, as they had shot my friend James Connelly in Dublin a few days previously. I resolved that whatever might happen I would go through with it.

The tension was relieved when we came out of Waverley Station into a raging snowstorm. A squad of tramway employees were working with crowbars, levering along a tram-car until it became connected with the cable. Like a crowd of school-boys, we stood and watched them at work.

It made me think we had arrived in Russia—an antiquated method of engineering and transport, a blinding snowstorm, and my emotions outraged at being lifted in the middle of the night without any charge preferred against me.

We wandered up to the Police Office. Captain Ross was awaiting us, and treated us with the greatest courtesy and kindness. He inquired where we were going to stay.

" You have the run of the city," he said, " so long as you do not go beyond the five-mile radius from here."

What were we to do ? We had been suddenly transferred to a strange city without any provision being made for us. We began to cudgel our brains as to where we would stay, for we had no money. Each of us thought of his different friends, but eventually four of us had no other resource than to march out to Morningside and seek shelter in the house of a friend of mine, John S. Clarke, later a colleague in the House of Commons.

In a small house, John S. Clarke lived with his wife and son and his mother. There was little room for anyone else, for the house was stacked up with antiquarian specimens, stuffed birds, animals, and other material that made it more like a museum than a dwelling-house!

To my great disappointment Clarke was not there. He was in Glasgow, where he had gone for the purpose of addressing a meeting, but had received a hint from a kindly policeman that he might be arrested if he went on with his meeting. He left the hall, passing on his way a bunch of detectives. He walked through them all easily by carrying his own hat. I know nobody who is so different without a hat. When John S. Clarke wears a hat, he is like a douce, Glasgow business man ; but he is so bald that, when he removes his hat, he looks like Grock, the clown!

Well, there we were, four of us, homeless, standing on the step of John Clarke's house. We had not long to wait, for without any hesitation we were taken in and accommodated, nominally until the return of the master of the house, but actually until we were in a fit condition financially to seek lodgings of our own.

It was while we were staying in Clarke's house that we had a pretty good revelation of the character of certain people. One evening we were in the I.L.P. hall when the lights were gradually lowered. Three times this happened. The third time they went out.

The Edinburgh people knew what it meant. They whispered : " Zeppelins ! "

Very silently we stole out into the pitch-dark streets. We walked to Morningside, a mile and a half, speaking in whispers, careful not to let our heels click too hard on the pavement. At last we reached the house where we were staying. Six of us entered. The only occupants were Mr Clarke's mother and her little grandson.

By midnight nothing had happened. Grandma and grandson went to bed. We remained talking of air-raids. One man was particularly talkative. He was a revolutionary who always talked in the most callous fashion of fighting, a man with brains but without morals of any kind. To me he was a blether. I paid little attention to his talk.

Suddenly a terrifying explosion occurred. Windows rattled, the ground quivered, pictures swung. We all gasped. I ran to the window and saw Vesuvius in eruption.

As I watched, I felt myself alone. Turning round, I found that my companions had run out of the house, even without putting on their boots. The door opened and the old lady appeared in a dressing-gown. At that moment another terrific explosion shook us. She said : " Oh, dear, I do hope the noise won't waken Sonnie ! "

I could not help smiling at her courage and care.

" It's probably all over now," I said.

She replied, " I hope so," and went off to bed again.

I opened the window. A great flash greeted me from the Castle and then, above the roaring, I heard the most dreadful screeching and shouting. The inmates in the Morningside Asylum had started pandemonium. Another bomb exploded, but nearer Leith, then another, followed by a fire.

When I was a young man I had read Dante's *Inferno*, which came out in parts at 4½*d.* each. Here it was in reality.

And the old lady in bed and the little boy slept peacefully through it all !

An hour later my friends came back one by one, all save the braggart. It was three in the morning before he appeared, fair oot o' his judgment a' thegither. He was frantic.

He told us he had seen the Zeppelin and had heard the Germans directing the gunners to shoot him.

" Ye must hae learnt German very quick," I said to him, but, while the others laughed, he went on raving.

That fellow turned up at the forty hours' strike. While some of us were being batoned, he cleared away, and, like Johnnie Cope, didn't stop running till he reached England.

A few years later he put all Britain into a panic.

They were weary days, brightened by occasional incidents. One day we visited Roslin Castle, and were entertained to tea by the chaplain, the Rev. R. C. Morrison, and his wife. He was a quiet, saint-like man who, though he hated our activities, nevertheless welcomed us to his table, and the " eight wild men from the Clyde " were as meek and gentle as schoolchildren at a Sunday-school party.

But we were not always meek and gentle !

One night at the Mound, Mrs Helen Crawfurd,

well known as militant suffragist, pacifist, and
Communist, was addressing a peace meeting as I
passed by.

After her, a man Kelly, very Irish, began to
speak, and received a rough handling. In the
crowd were two Australian soldiers, huge men.
They were violent in their barracking. I noticed
one of them stoop down, take off a spur, and begin
to fix it round his hand. Forgetting that I was
forbidden to attend public meetings, I made a dive
at him.

There was almost a fight, but when I told the
crowd what I had seen, they called out : " Dirty ! "
The soldiers slipped away, and then the crowd
turned on Kelly. He was badly mauled and
hustled along Princes Street toward the Calton
Jail.

It was obvious there was going to be serious
trouble, so I pushed through the crowd and shouted:
" Stand back, there ! " I caught hold of Kelly by
the collar and said : " I arrest you for causing a
breach of the peace."

I bundled him into a cab, and was well away
before the crowd discovered that they had been
tricked.

Another of our interests was to go to Calton Hill,
overlooking the Jail, and wave to James Maxton,
William Gallacher, John W. Muir, Walter Bell, and
James McDougall when they came into the yard
for exercise.

Let it be said in honour of the good-nature of
their jailers that, when it was discovered that we
were sending greetings, the officers found something

to attract their attention elsewhere for that one precious minute a day. It was an open secret that every one in Calton Jail learned to love James Maxton.

After four months, during which there had been no disturbance and no breaking of the bond, the authorities began to press us to take up engineering work in England. The temptation was strong, for engineers were making big money, while we were dependent on the kindness of our friends.

One by one the deportees were fixed up in England. I refused. For me it was Beardmore's or nothing. I told the Military that I had not come to Edinburgh of my own free will. They had brought me there, and there I would stay till they took me back. They became more insistent when I told them that, through the aid of the Clyde Workers' Committee, I had set up house in Edinburgh and brought my wife and family to stay with me.

That house became a rendezvous.

One day two hundred Clyde shop stewards came through to see me and make a presentation to me. We marched along Princes Street to a *café* at the Post Office.

The Military Command began to grow uneasy. They wanted me out of Edinburgh. They offered me a job in charge of a shell factory in Woolwich. I refused. They came back with tempting offers in Sheffield and Coventry. I said : " Beardmore's or nowhere."

Sam Bunten, then my Trade Union chief, now a Government official, came through to persuade me.

" If you don't go to England," he said, " you will go to Calton Jail."

" All right," I said, " but I will go nowhere of my free will except Beardmore's. I will fight this thing through to the bitter end."

I found it more difficult to resist my old friend, George Lansbury. He begged me to fall in with the others and take a job in England.

When I refused, he went up to the Military Headquarters to see what could be done. He returned and said I should have to go, because he had seen written evidence more than sufficient to have me put up against a wall.

That made me more determined than ever. There was nothing against me. Who could have sent written evidence? There could be no evidence, except a fabrication. It had never been mentioned to me, although I visited the Scottish Command Headquarters every week and was put through my paces by Colonel Levita and Major Gardner.

These two were always trying to pump me. I refused to be pumped. Anyway, there was no water in the pump. They had somehow got it into their heads that there was a great treasonable or seditious organization on the Clyde. Dr Addison had even said so in the House of Commons. I had never heard of such a thing and I told the Military so, but they refused to believe me. The fact is that they had people employed to supply reports on " how the wind blew." Like other spies, they had to earn their wages, and invented the story of rebellion on the Clyde for which there was not one shred of foundation. But at that time lies were more popular than truth and rumours more acceptable than reality.

The pressure on the part of the Military Authorities to persuade me to sign a document to be of good behaviour increased. Each of the documents implied an admission on my part that I had been guilty of impeding the production of munitions. I refused to sign. Nor would I write a letter asking to be liberated. Why should I? I had not asked to be deported from Glasgow. I would not ask as a favour what I demanded as a right.

A few days after my meeting with Mr Lansbury, I was called to the Headquarters of the Scottish Command. Colonel Levita said to me :

" You must sign a document in mild terms and return to Glasgow. I am the man who has the power. I have 50,000 troops. I am the man to give the order to fire."

That was almost a threat. It was necessary that we should understand each other. Colonel Levita had always treated me well.

" I think you had better understand my position once and for all. Until I am restored to my wife and family with all my rights, I will go nowhere and I will decide nothing.

" Give me my freedom and, as soon as I am a free man, I will decide what to do. Until then, I remain here."

What a country ! Imagine such a series of incidents and such a scene in any other country ! It is incredible. Had I been anywhere but in

Britain, I should have been quietly dispatched as a nuisance or a traitor ! Nuisance I may have been. Traitor I never was.

Sometimes some of my colleagues wonder when I speak of this land in the way I do. I have most reason to know that it is in very truth the land of the brave and the free, for these soldiers were brave men, but they respected freedom. As I remember them in the days of anxiety and over-work, I send them greetings. I had troubled them much. They were to stand a lot more trouble from me before the finish. They were soldiers. I was a civilian. They were on top for the time being. But they never forgot that we were all British. They played the game in the British way and I hope they think the same of me.

Their attitude as Military Authorities is set out in clear British fashion in the instructions of General Sir Spencer Ewart, Commander-in-Chief, Scottish Command, to Colonel Levita. He said he was most anxious there should be no military pressure or punishment inflicted in a Labour trouble, and added : " We must have quiet. Do what you can to keep these men away. Let them go where they like. I am not going to take a hand in a Labour trouble. It is not for me to say whether either side is right or wrong, whatever the grievances of either employer or employed may be. All I am con-cerned in is that it is my duty to see that the output of munitions is not interfered with." Only they arrested me and left Sir William Beardmore in Parkhead.

Nine months had passed since my deportation.

During that time I had done no work. But more and more the eyes of the British engineers were centred on me. They felt that I had been badly treated by the Government and by the Trade Union.

In January 1917 the Labour Party Conference was to be held in Manchester. The engineers in Scotland had the right to send a delegate. Sixteen candidates were nominated for the position. I received more votes than the other fifteen put together. I was not on parole and I determined that I was going to Manchester.

A beautiful scheme was arranged. I was to dress myself as a minister, leave Edinburgh on the quiet, go down to Manchester, and appear in that garb in the Conference in order to challenge the Executive to take up my case and have me restored to Glasgow.

Just when everything was ready, I was summoned to the Military Headquarters. Colonel Levita was waiting for me.

I asked what he wanted me for. He looked me up and down and said :

" I was just wondering how you would look if you were dressed like a Nonconformist minister."

I soon found that he knew our arrangements to the last detail.

Even among us there was a spy ! Staggered as I was, I could not help laughing. Then he said :

" Your elaborate disguise will be quite unnecessary. I recognize the importance of the great vote you have received from the engineers. You may go to the Conference, but you must return to Edinburgh."

" I will go back to Glasgow," I said.

He dared me to do it, and I said we would see.

On arrival at Manchester I had a conference with Ramsay MacDonald, John Wheatley, and Tom Johnston. I told them I was going to challenge the Conference to take up my case and then go back to Glasgow.

They all approved of the idea, but Ramsay MacDonald warned me that, if it came off, it would be all right, but, if I failed, it would be bad for every one, and prison for me.

" Then I am going to Glasgow or to prison," I said.

At the Conference, through the kindness of Mr J. T. Brownlie and Mr George N. Barnes, I was allowed an opening by being put up, instead of Brownlie, to second a resolution regarding the Trade Union agreements governing the working of a certain machine.

Having formally seconded the resolution, I told the Conference the story of the deportation. They listened in silence. At the end I said :

" No charge has been made against us ; no trial has been offered us. On my return I shall have no means of life but labour. I am no criminal. If I break the law in future, I must be dealt with as other men. To-day for the first time I have the opportunity to place my case before the representatives of British Labour.

" Having done so, I place it on your shoulders with all its responsibilities. Great principles of constitutional liberty are challenged. You must defend them. When I leave this Conference I will not go back to deportation. I go home to Glasgow or I go to prison."

The effect is best told by Ramsay Mac-Donald, who described the scene in *Forward*: " If nothing else happened, this incident would have redeemed the Conference. During it, the Conference went back to its fundamental emotions of freedom, independence, and hostility to the present governing classes. The delegates, after one of those silent pauses when the mind is grasping what has happened, burst out into a tornado of cheers. Thank you very much, Clyde engineers, for helping some of us to retain our faith in the Labour Movement by giving us a chance to see what the heart of that Movement is."

After the " tornado of cheering," the delegates carried me shoulder-high. The Conference adjourned. A telegram was sent to Mr Lloyd George.

The next afternoon thousands of munition workers gathered outside the hall to bid me Godspeed as I went off to Glasgow or to prison. No conqueror ever had a greater triumphal procession.

I returned to Glasgow. My wife and family had returned from Edinburgh when I set out for Manchester. It was the first time I had been home for nine months.

On Sunday morning I was feeling very ill, and lay in bed. Two friends were with me in the kitchen, when two Glasgow detectives came in. They were very nice, and said they wanted to speak to me privately, and that my two friends had better go out. My friends rose to go, but I said :

" No, no. Whatever you have to say to me, say it from the housetops. There are no secrets here. This is my home, and they are not going out of here for you."

" All right, Mr Kirkwood, but we have been sent by the Scottish Command to obtain your signature to this paper. This is not a civil affair. It is military, and you must either sign it or come with us."

It was not the first of the many documents I was asked to sign. They were growing milder and milder. I read the document through. It was a declaration that " in future " I would do nothing to impede the production of munitions. I had not done so. On the contrary, I had accelerated the process. I said : " I am sorry I cannot sign this."

The detectives said they didn't want to do anything to me, and were sure I did not want to get them into trouble. I agreed. They asked for my word of honour not to leave the house for twenty-four hours. I gave them my word, and I kept it. Twenty-four hours passed, and forty-eight, and seventy-two—no sign of the police. I thought I was free. On the fourth day I went into Glasgow with John Wheatley. We met Tom Johnston, and it finished up with me being packed off in my best clothes with bag and umbrella to Crieff Hydropathic.

It was a new experience for me. I had never before been in a hydropathic or any similar resort of the well-to-do. I was astonished to find that, as the old woman said, " the place was fair polluted

10

wi' meenisters." It was like a ministers' guest-house. I was still more surprised in the evening to see the ministers and their lady friends dancing or sitting at a dozen tables, playing cards ! So innocent was I of the fashionable world that I thought ministers looked upon card-playing as a sin and a folly. I could not play cards. I thought it strange to have dancing and card-playing during the War.

In the morning, after a very good breakfast, I attended a religious service in the reading-room. It " soothed my savage breast and tamed my heart of fire." I remember singing both the psalm and the hymn with great gusto. I felt friendly towards the people.

After the service a girl went over to the organ and began to play. I sat on, alone, entranced by the music.

Suddenly a hand was laid on my shoulder and a voice said : " Are you David Kirkwood, the deportee from the Clyde?" I said : "I am." I was told I was wanted in the Medical Superintendent's office.

As I reached the office, I saw that it was flanked by soldiers. They had come for me at last. The Chief Constable of the County stood at attention. We had a long confabulation and then the Chief Constable said :

" You will have to come with me down to the Police Office. These soldiers are going to take you to Edinburgh Castle by the first train."

" All right," I said, " but I'll need to go upstairs for my bag and my umbrella."

The Chief Constable came upstairs with me. My room was on the fifth floor. The Hydro is built on a rise, and there are hills all round. When we reached my room, I walked to the window and said : " Look at that lovely country. Isn't it beautiful ? "

The Chief Constable looked, and said he had no idea that Crieff was such a beautiful place and that he had never seen it from such a height. Then he turned to me and said :

" Kirkwood, you're a queer fish. I can't make you out at all. If I were you, I should have something more on my mind than looking at the ordinary things of Nature."

They took me from the Hydro by a back door, lest I should give the place a bad name or disturb the peace of mind of the ministers.

At the Police Office I was to be put in a cell. I refused to go.

" I am not your prisoner," I said. " I am in the charge of the Military. I will wait here for the train to Edinburgh."

I was given permission to telegraph to my wife the news of my next point of rest.

I must have been in the police-station for two or three hours, treated with the utmost kindness and goodwill. One of Britain's greatest achievements is the creation of a police force which performs its duty with efficiency and retains an attitude of detachment. After three hours I was hungry, and was offered tea and bread and butter.

" No, thank you," I said. " No tea and bread and butter for me ! I want steak, potatoes and a vegetable, and then a pudding."

They roared with laughter.

These things were sent for, and a fine Scots lassie brought them in. I enjoyed my dinner.

The train arrived. The Chief Constable shook hands and wished me good luck, and with my soldier escort I boarded the train.

In little more than an hour I was in a dungeon in Edinburgh Castle, sitting on my bag, with my umbrella propped up in a corner!

CHAPTER XII

The Victim

THE Castle of Edinburgh is of great age. It was built at a time when oppression drove the people to rebellion and then cruelly crushed the rebellious.

My new habitation was a vault far below the ground, into which the only light entered from a small grated window high up near the roof. Above my vault were the guards' quarters, occupied by German and Austrian officer-prisoners. They were a noisy crew, singing, shouting, and scrapping day and night. They seemed to want for nothing.

I thought it strange that I, who was innocent of any offence, should be in a dungeon while the captured enemy should be so cheerfully housed up above.

I was a done man. My mind refused to think. My body seemed incapable of exertion. I wondered what was to happen next.

Hours passed in utter loneliness.

The little light faded from the window. I was alone in the darkness. Sitting there, elbows on knees and cheeks in the cup of my hands, I seemed the most helpless of mortals. I was very near to breaking-point.

But, as I sat, the tears quietly came to my eyes, trickled down my cheeks into my hands, found their way round my wrists and lost themselves in my sleeves. They were to me a physical, mental, and spiritual ventilation.

When, an hour later, the door opened and a soldier appeared, Richard was himself again. In the light of the soldier's lamp I saw my bed, a mattress and a pillow. They were filthy.

" What kin' o' way is that to treat a man ? " I asked. " I cudna sleep on the like o' that."

The soldier looked and shook his head.

" Indeed, no," he said in a Highland accent. " That wouldn't do at all. No ! No ! " and promptly turned the mattress and flyped [1] the pillow-slip.

He left me food that gied me a scunner.[2] But I was too spent to worry myself with food. As soon as he left, I lay down and slept.

For fourteen days that vault was my home. I had no letters and no friendly callers. But I had others.

On the third day a soldier swung open the door and stood looking at me. He laid his hand on his hip.

" D'ye see that ? " he asked. He gave his hip a slap. " D'ye ken whit that is ? "

" Ay, a revolver."

" Ye're richt. It's a revolver, an' it's loaded an', let me tell ye, I'd raither use it to shoot you nor a German. You're David Kirkwood o' the Clyde."

I thought he was either half intoxicated or off

---

[1] Turned inside out.—Ed.　　　[2] Made me feel sick.—Ed.

his balance. The guard would not be changed for two hours. I did not know what to do, as he rambled on. Then he quoted the Bible.

That gave me an opening. I quoted a text against his. He quoted another, and soon we were in the thick of a Bible talk, matching text with text. It was a real Scottish ' crack.' At last he mentioned God's Chosen People. That gave me my chance.

I slowly narrated the history of the Jews, of Abraham and Lot, the building of the altar at Hebron, of Lot's wife, of Isaac and Esau and Jacob. Then came my favourite story of Joseph. I was grateful to Joseph—he occupied fully twenty minutes ! Then we passed to Pharaoh and Moses, and the very pleasant story of the mother who made Pharaoh's daughter pay her for being a nurse to her own child. After that it was easy to tramp through the desert, though it took the Israelites forty days and forty nights. By the time we had reached the Land of Promise, in which I was more fortunate than Moses, I was becoming exhausted, but I was grateful to the minister whose Bible class I had attended in my youth !

It was easy for me to judge that the Bible and the things of the Bible were the soldier's greatest interest. He was more interested in the Bible than in shooting me, although he had come for that purpose. I have often noticed that people who are attracted by the blood stories of the Old Testament are inclined to look upon weapons of destruction as instruments confided to their care for carrying out what they believe to be the purposes of the Almighty.

It is a kind of brain affection that has put a blight on religion through the ages.

Our talk lasted over an hour. There was still an hour to go. I told him about the origins of wars, then about myself and the trouble at Parkhead, keeping him interested.

At last the guard was changed. As he went away, I said he would maybe yet learn that this was a capitalist war and find himself without a job.

Many years later I was speaking at an open-air meeting in Denny when a man came forward and shook me by the hand.

" D'ye no' remember me, Mr Kirkwood ? " he asked.

I said : " I'm awfully sorry, but I don't, though there's something familiar about your voice."

" D'ye no' remember in Edinburgh Castle a soldier who wanted to shoot ye ? "

Instantly the whole scene came into my mind and, pointing to him, I exclaimed :

" Thou art the man ! "

" Ay," he said ; " and ye didna know it, but ye converted me that day."

He was now under the New Dispensation.

The morning after the shooting incident I was ordered to leave my cell and empty the ash-bins.

" D'ye no' see I'm in my Sunday claes," I said. " I'll dae naethin' o' the sort."

An hour later I was ordered to carry coals to the officers' quarters. Again I refused, saying : " I'm no' a coal-heaver. I'm an engineer."

A little later Colonel Levita came in.

" Now, Kirkwood," he said, " I've come to give you an opportunity to get clear of all this, honourably. All you have to do is to sign this paper. Read it over. Put your name to it and you are a free man without a stain on your character."

He handed me a typewritten document. It was a modified form of the one I had been asked to sign in Glasgow. I refused. He called me pig-headed and said that not a hand had been lifted to help me, that I was alone and would soon be forgotten.

My gorge rose, and I gave him a bit of my mind.

" You may be the head of the Army and the Navy, but you are no gentleman. Here am I alone, and you, a Brigadier-General, bullying me, your prisoner. You can do what you like with me, but I will not sign."

He then took from his pocket a letter written in his own hand, very mild compared with the others. He told me he had a great regard for me. He told me that he was being superseded by Colonel Guest, and said that we were brothers in affliction. Then he added :

" To show you I'm a gentleman, I am not asking you to do what I would not do myself. I am taking the insult without challenge. When the War is over, your wrongs will be righted. Will you sign ? "

I refused.

Another officer came in. They pressed me again. I said :

" Put me back in Parkhead, but I will sign nothing."

I was all out. They were excited and indignant. They left my cell and, in their anger, they left the two documents. I have kept them ever since.

An hour later Colonel Levita came back and said :

" Kirkwood, I have decided to let you out of the Castle, but you are still a deportee."

He left me without another word.

The door was open. No soldier was on guard. Having packed my attaché-case, I took my pot-hat and my umbrella and walked out into the open air. I had signed nothing.

Making my way to Melbourne Hall, I found John S. Clarke, who fixed me up with lodgings and told me that James Maxton, William Gallacher, and James McDougall were all out of jail and had been sent by the Clyde Workers' Committee to Moffat Hydropathic, whither I was to follow them.

That was a strange fortnight.

On arrival at Moffat Station, the Chief Constable met me. How did he know I was coming ? He saluted and said : " Good afternoon, Mr Kirk-wood." It was a most generous greeting. I raised my hat and said : " Good afternoon, Chief." It was like Stanley's meeting with Livingstone in Africa. The Chief Constable ought to have said : " Mr Kirkwood, I presume ? " He turned away and I went on to the Hydropathic—the second time I had been in such a place.

Gallacher was blooming as usual. McDougall was melancholy. Maxton was ill with hiccough —constant, uncontrollable hiccough—a dreadful malady to have. He had not seen a doctor. I insisted on taking him to a Dr Park, who sounded him and found the cause of the trouble in the stomach, not the heart.

While he was doing his work, Dr Park gave us the greatest telling-off of James Maxton and David Kirkwood that ever I heard. " Traitor of the deepest dye," he called Kirkwood, and said Maxton was a vagabond. It was a good thing they were both safe within the walls of Edinburgh Castle. We kept back our laughter with difficulty. As we were saying our good-byes, Jimmie said, pointing to me :

" This is the traitor of the deepest dye."

" And this," I said, " is the vagabond, though he's mair like a scarecrow nor a Russian revolutionary."

Dr Park got a sad drop. Like so many people who thought they hated us, he did not hate us. What he hated was his own idea of us. Even when he found out, he was not antagonistic.

We all laughed and parted in friendship.

The Hydropathic was full of wounded officers. It was tragic to see them, splendid men, hobbling about. Of course they knew who we were, but they paid no attention to us. They gave a good example of self-control, for I am sure that in their distress they must have hated us.

In all the fortnight only two of them spoke to us.

One was a Cameron Highlander. He was in his cups. He came over to our table full of insulting remarks. We paid no attention. Then he ruffled Maxton's hair, saying : " Look at his hair. He's more of a Frenchman than a Scot." That was too much for me.   I rose up and said : " Look here, Captain, if you don't go over to your own table, I'll smash your jaw for you, and the whole British Army won't protect ye."   He gave a silly wave of the hand and went away like a child. The other officers looked, but said nothing.

The other meeting did not end so well for me. A young lieutenant, a real Apollo for beauty, took me aside and said he was in great trouble.   His allowance had not come and he was being threatened by a merchant.   Would I let him have £4 for three days.   I had £5.   I gave him £4. An hour later the Hydro was in an uproar.   The police had come to arrest the lieutenant.   He had got money from many people with his story and his pleading way.   He had done several other things as well.

Captain Ross, the Chief Constable of Edinburgh, wanted me to make a charge, but I refused.   It was not for me to crush a young fellow who was probably off his head.

On my return to Edinburgh I settled down in the rooms of Mrs Ross, who was in the habit of having student lodgers.

In May 1917 I received word that my wife was very ill.   Her time was near, I knew.   I wondered if I should ask leave to go through to Glasgow.   Or need I ask leave ?   It was so little I had to sign.   I could not ask leave without signing and I would not sign.   I was still cogitating when a telegram came from my son that he had a wee sister. Then I was neither to bind nor to hold. I ran to the Scottish Command. In Princes Street I met Mr William Adamson, M.P., and a group of Fife delegates going to a conference, and told him what had happened. At that time Adamson was not friendly with me. He believed what others had said about me and, being ardently pro-War, he regarded me as a nuisance, if not worse. But he promised he would go to the Scottish Command and that I should be released.

At the Scottish Command I found Major Gardner, erect, spruce, and cropped. Levita had gone. I was told he had been succeeded by Colonel Guest. Then the story he had told me in my cell was true after all. I had thought he was bluffing.

I was taken in to Colonel Guest. He was kindness itself. If I would sign one of the letters, he was sure he could get me to Glasgow. I refused. He asked me to give up Levita's letter. I refused to let it out of my possession.

We talked.

At last he said : " Mr Kirkwood, I am a married man, and you may rely on me doing all I can to let you go home. But I must consult London. Come at six to-night."

That was a terrible afternoon. So sure was I that it would be all right that I went to my lodging and packed my bag. I bought a ticket for Glasgow —a single ! At five o'clock I set out with bag and umbrella for the Scottish Command.

At six o'clock I was told that London had intimated that on no account was I to be allowed to leave Edinburgh until I signed the letter. Then I burst out. I called them brutes. I told Major Gardner he was a Death's Head Uhlan.

" You must not speak like that here ! " shouted Colonel Guest.

What did I care ?

" To-morrow this will be raised on the floor of the House of Commons," I said.

I marched over to the Post Office and telephoned to William Adamson in his office in Dunfermline.

" All right, my cullan," he said. " I'm just leaving for London."

Back at my lodgings, I passed the time writing letters to Robert Smillie, John Wheatley, Tom Johnston, and Rosslyn Mitchell. Then I walked up and down like a caged lion. The hours went very slowly. It was nearly midnight when I heard men's voices at the door.

" Is this where David Kirkwood, the deported engineer, stays ? " one asked.

My landlady said, " Oh, no ! " But I was at the door, where soldiers were standing.

" Dearie me ! " said the flustered Mrs Ross. " I've heard of Civil Engineers and Marine Engineers, but never of Deportment Engineers."

A motor-car was waiting. The soldiers said they had been sent for me. We drove away, and, to my horror, the car went into Waverley Station. Had something happened to my wife ? The thought filled my heart with hatred.

The station was in darkness. I saw the shadow of a whole company of soldiers standing at attention. Out of the gloom stepped a great six-footer, in full regimentals. It was Colonel Guest.

" I've come to take you to see your wife," he said. " I've a special train here, and I'm going with you."

This seemed to confirm my fear. I stood transfixed and said : " If anything has happened to my wife, I'll hae your life or you'll hae mine."

" No, no, everything's all right," he said, but I did not believe him. I thought he was breaking the news gently.

Never did a brass-hat have a more morose companion. We sat, the only passengers in the train, and neither of us spoke.

At Queen Street, Glasgow, the station seemed to be full of soldiers, all drawn up in parade order. It was now one o'clock in the morning. Glasgow was silent and dark.

I was led to a motor-car in front of which were two soldiers. Colonel Guest sat beside me. We drove to my home. At the close-mouth he stopped and, in the gentlest way, said :

" I think you had better go upstairs by yourself. If I appear in these regimentals, it might give Mrs Kirkwood a shock. Go up and see how things are, and then come down and let me know."

I ran up three steps at a time and chapped on the door in the way we both knew so well. Then I pushed open the letter-box and heard my wife say :

" There's Davie at the door."

I think in all my life I have never heard anything so wonderful as that phrase.

I found my wife with the baby by her side. They were both well and comfortable. After a little talk, I said I'd have to go down and tell the man who had brought me through.

As I came down the stairs, Colonel Guest was standing in the close-mouth. In his fawn " British warm " and his red-banded cap, he looked colossal.

" Well ? " he asked.

" Everything is all right, sir," I said. " My wife's fine and the child is just splendid."

Then occurred a scene which I shall remember till my dying day.

Colonel Guest stepped back, looked at me for a second, then threw his arms about me and gave me a hug as he said :

" Kirkwood, you are a man. Many a one would have come down with a cock-and-bull story. You come down and tell me everything is all right. I am going to leave you here at home. I'm doing it on my own responsibility, but I'll leave you until I get in touch with Headquarters."

I was speechless. We looked at each other. We clasped hands. He saluted, and moved away to his car in the darkness. I waved to him as he went—

> For there is neither East nor West, border
>   nor breed nor birth,
> When two strong men stand face to face, though
>   they come from the ends of the earth.

Then I went upstairs. I was home again !
For how long was it to be this time, I wondered ?
Two days later I received a letter from Colonel

Guest informing me that I was at liberty to remain in Glasgow during my wife's illness. A week later I received another letter extending the liberty until the end of May.

In the interval a peculiar event had happened. The Final Appeal Court of the Amalgamated Society of Engineers was due to hold its triennial meeting in Glasgow—the most important meeting of the Society. We called it the House of Lords. To this court representatives came from all the British Dominions.

I had been proposed as a delegate to the court, but the officials at Headquarters had been able to exclude me under a rule that no delegate could be appointed unless he had been working at the trade for the full year before the meetings. I had been deported for fourteen months. On that ground they held I had not been working at the trade—a miserable technicality invented to keep me away.

When the delegates met, it followed that David Lowe, as chairman of the district in which the court was to sit, was to be chairman of the court. The delegates had other ideas, not out of any feeling of disrespect for David Lowe, but to demonstrate their confidence in me, and, against the wishes of the bosses and against all precedent, appointed me chairman. I was not present at the meeting, not being a delegate.

Poor Robert Young (now Sir Robert Young), the General Secretary, who had turned me down as a delegate, had to telegraph to the Government to let me leave Edinburgh in order that I might preside over his Conference. And all the time I was in Glasgow, ignorant of the doings of the Conference, for I was at my home, liberated until May 31st.

On May 29th I received a telegram from the Scottish Command :

> General Officer Commanding-in-Chief Scottish Command is pleased to grant extension of permission to reside in Glasgow so as to enable you to accept Chairmanship of Final Appeal Court—COLONEL GUEST, *General Staff Officer, Scottish Command.*

The morning after, I received a letter from Colonel Guest :

> HEADQUARTERS
> SCOTTISH COMMAND
> EDINBURGH
> *30th May, 1917*
>
> SIR,
>   I am directed to inform you that the General Officer Commanding-in-Chief, Scottish Command, has revoked the Order against you dated 25th March, 1916, whereby you were not permitted to reside in Glasgow.
>   I am, Sir,
>   Yours faithfully,
>   H. GUEST,
>   *Lieut.-Colonel, General Staff, Scottish Command*

I was free again ! I had signed nothing. I had promised nothing. I seemed to hear my father saying : " Never heed, ma cullan, we'll win through yet."

For three weeks I was kept busy with the A.S.E. Appeal Court. When that closed, I was free but unemployed. I could not be satisfied until I was reinstated in Beardmore's.

CHAPTER XIII

I Appeal to Cæsar

WHEN the Labour Party resolves to hold an inquiry, it does it thoroughly. At the Annual Conference of the Party held at Manchester in January 1917, at which I made a somewhat dramatic and unexpected appearance, it was resolved to appoint a Special Committee " to report upon the circumstances which resulted in the Deportation in March 1916 of David Kirkwood and other workmen employed in the Munition Factories in the Clyde District."

The Committee was representative in character and thorough in action. At meetings in London and Glasgow over sixty persons gave evidence, including Sir Lynden Macassey, K.C., Lieutenant-Colonel C. B. Levita, M.V.O., and Mr Arthur Henderson. The Report, which reads like a State document and fills sixty-three pages of close print, was a complete vindication of my character as a man and an engineer. The Committee gave me a rap over the knuckles for disregarding the officials of the Trade Union, but they had nothing to say against me in connexion with the strike, and put the blame where it belonged, on the management of the Works.

Vindicated by the withdrawal of the Deportation Order and by the Report of the Special Committee of the Labour Party, I was still unemployed. I had many offers of employment, but by this time I had become so much driven into myself that reinstatement in Beardmore's had become an obsession with me.

I resolved to appeal unto Cæsar—Cæsar in this case being the Rt. Hon. Winston Churchill, M.P., Minister of Munitions.

To that end I went to London. The natural thing to do was to get in touch with Ramsay MacDonald. By this time we were on terms of deep friendship. Three times he had come through to Edinburgh to see me. Together we had roamed the Pentland Hills, and in those tramps he had opened his heart to me in a way that few men have ever done.

" By the rivers of Babylon there we sat down, yea, we wept when we remembered Zion."

The War had killed Keir Hardie. It had made Ramsay MacDonald a broken-hearted man. It seemed as if he was doomed to spend his life tending goats in the wilderness while the Tory sheep munched grass in green and pleasant pastures.

But the friendship of Members of Parliament is a wonderful thing. I did not understand it then. I was to learn it later on and to become a sharer of it in full measure.

To my surprise, Ramsay MacDonald, in agreement with the idea that I should see Winston Churchill, promptly went to the telephone and, while I waited, arranged a meeting for that afternoon in the Hotel Metropole, the headquarters of the Ministry.

It has always been a cause of wonder to me how the busiest men manage to squeeze in time for something unexpected—and then appear to have nothing else on hand at the moment.

I had formed an opinion of Winston Churchill as a daring, reckless, swashbuckler individual who was afraid of no one. I felt that if I could win him there was nothing he would not do.

But I was very critical of him. I expected arrogance, military precision, abruptness. When he appeared, I knew I was wrong. He came in, his fresh face all smiles, and greeted me simply, without a trace of side or trappings. I felt I had found a friend.

" How do you do, Mr Kirkwood? I have heard a good deal about you," he said.

" I dare say you have," I replied.

" Yes, and I want you to know that, whatever happens, nothing is to be allowed to stand in the way of the production of the munitions of war."

" Quite right," I said.

Then he rang a bell, saying : " Let's have a cup of tea and a bit of cake together."

What a difference so small a thing can make ! I remembered in that instant the awful hours I had waited for Lloyd George and Lynden Macassey, and my feeling at the time : " If only they would give us a cup of tea ! "

Here was the man, supposed never to think of trifles, suggesting tea and cake—a sort of bread and salt of friendship. It was magnificent. We debated over the teacups.

" Well, what about it ? " he asked.

" I will tell you," I replied. " The Government deported me without cause. I have had redress for those wrongs. I realize that what was done to me was done because we were at war. ' I waive the quantum o' the sin ' "—at which he screwed up his face—" but I am unemployed. I am a highly skilled engineer, idle since May. I want you to put me back in Beardmore's whether Beardmore wants me or not."

I have seldom seen a man look so astonished. His brows came down. He looked at me and said :

" Look here, Kirkwood, you have a great reputation, but you are not living up to it. I expected you to be a reasonable man. You are the most unreasonable man I ever met in all my life. Here am I, three weeks in my job, and you ask me to put you back in Beardmore's whether he wants you or not, into the Works he has built up over a lifetime."

" Yes, that is so," I said. " It may seem a strange request. I've told you I have forgiven all that was done to me, but this is doing it all over again. I am treated as if I was a traitor to my country. There is no worse injury could be done to a Scotsman. You have got to do this thing or I'll go out from here and from the Isle of Wight to John o' Groats I'll advocate a down-tool policy. . . ."

He whipped round with flashing eyes : " You

must not mention that here, Kirkwood. I will not tolerate it. Remember you are in the Ministry of Munitions."

" I would say it, Mr Churchill, were it in the Court of Heaven, and not only say it, sir, but I'm going to do it."

He sat back in his chair, looked straight into my eyes and roared with laughter. Then he said :

" By Jove, and I believe you would ! But there's no good in getting heated about it. You feel wronged and only one thing can change that feeling. Well, why not ? Let us see what we can do in the next two or three days, and it won't be my fault if you are not back in Beardmore's."

I knew something of what that meant. I knew I had talked with a man of great ability, great courage, and great power, character written in every wrinkle of his face. I knew that he was a man whose word would not be broken.

I came back to Glasgow to find three offers of employment in Glasgow. I refused them all.

On the third day I was summoned to Parkhead, where Mr Charles Pelmier, General Manager of Beardmore's shell factories, offered me a job in the Mile-end Shell Factory. I accepted.

" Is it workman or manager ? " I asked.

" Manager," he said.

We shook hands.

" I'll keep my word," I said, " but I should like to engage some of my friends, fine engineers, who are not working."

" Whatever you do, you do on your own responsibility."

Thus it came that in Mile-end Shell Factory, with David Kirkwood as foreman, worked David Hanton, William Gallacher, and wee MacManus as shop stewards.

What a team ! There never was anything like it in Great Britain. We organized a bonus system in which every one benefited by high production.

Records were made only to be broken. The factory, built for a 12,000 output, produced 24,000. In six weeks we held the record for output in Great Britain, and we never lost our premier position.

Sir William Beardmore came often to see the system working. He announced one day that the manager of the department which did the best output would get a present of the best hat in Glasgow. That hat was mine ! When I was announced the winner, he drove up in his car. We went into town chatting all the way, and in R. W. Forsyth's he presented me with a fine Austrian velour bonnet. Indeed, he gave me two, for a year later I sent it in to be cleaned. It was lost. I was given a new one. Six weeks later, my own was found and sent to me with compliments !

Indirectly that hat helped Ramsay MacDonald. When he went to Aberavon, he was criticized for having associated with me, "a traitor." He told the story of the hat I won from Beardmore, and that finished the criticism.

Until the Armistice I held that job. I took not an hour off. But in my spare time at the week-ends I roamed England and Scotland, addressing meetings in favour of peace by negotiation.

The Independent Labour Party was at the

zenith of its influence. We were all scorned and laughed at—MacDonald, Snowden, Bruce Glazier, Clifford Allan, Wheatley, Johnston, Maxton, and Dollan. But the people flocked to our meetings.

Fourteen days after the Armistice, Parliament was dissolved. Lloyd George and Bonar Law began the " Coupon " election. I had over twenty invitations to stand for Parliament. I chose Dumbarton Burghs. The constituency consists of the two towns, Dumbarton and Clydebank.

The election began with five candidates in the field : Mr Ridge-Bedell, Conservative ; Mr Ford, a schoolmaster in the district, Liberal ; Mr Peacock, Independent ; Provost Taylor of Clydebank, Coalition ; and myself, Socialist. In a few days Provost Taylor received the " Coupon," and the others folded their tents like the Arabs and as silently stole away.

In that election the Socialists went down like ninepins. The country had only one hero, Lloyd George, and only one object : " Make the Germans pay."

I received the largest number of votes ever cast in Scotland for a Socialist candidate, but I did not get in. Only Neil MacLean and Duncan Graham were elected in the West of Scotland. An amusing scene took place at one of my meetings. The manager of John Brown's of Clydebank made a bitter attack on me, stating that I was a slacker, a rebel, and no better than a corner boy. He also wrote to the local paper telling the town what he thought about me, which was not much.

Of their own initiative, four of the foremen I had worked with in Beardmore's wrote a letter contradicting every statement made by my attacker, and offering to come to Clydebank and speak at one of my meetings. Such a chance was not to be missed. We advertised a great demonstration in the Town Hall. It was besieged. When I came on to the platform with my quartette of stalwart bodyguard, the crowd rose as one man. But what a fiasco ! One by one these honest sons of toil were called upon to speak. None of them could say a word. They were in a stage-panic. At last one of them said quite loud, as we were accustomed to speak in the roar of machinery : " Ye'd better speak for us yersel, Davie." The audience saw the fun of the thing and burst into laughter and cheering. I had to tell them that, " on behalf of my four friends from Beardmore's," I would now read the character of " their friend, David Kirkwood."

It was in this atmosphere of defeat that there arose a new movement called the " Soldiers', Sailors', and Workers' Council." In Russia, Kerensky's *bourgeois* revolution had collapsed. The mysterious Lenin and the egocentric and efficient Trotsky proclaimed the Bolshevik Republic. It began with " Soldiers', Sailors', and Workers' Councils," the forerunner of the Soviet Republic and the Union of Soviet Republics.

In Glasgow we formed the new Council on the model of the Soviet.

We arranged a great demonstration at which Ramsay MacDonald, against the advice of Philip

Snowden, came to speak. But D.O.R.A. intervened. The meeting was proclaimed.

Forbidden the hall, we held the meeting in the open air at McNeil Street. I have never heard Ramsay MacDonald so violent as he was at that meeting. He cast discretion to the four winds of heaven. He had lost his seat in Parliament. He was suffering from the outrage of the " Coupon " election.

The Soldiers', Sailors', and Workers' Council died an unnatural death. It was choked by its own excesses. It was more Bolshevik than the Bolsheviks. The workers laughed and went on with their jobs.

It was not long before the jobs stopped. Shell factories closed down. Thousands were paid off every week. Soon the savings began to dwindle.

Some of us thought it would be a good idea to share what work there was by reducing the hours of labour. Representatives of various crafts met to discuss procedure. In accordance with our plan, the engineers demanded a forty-hour week. It was refused. A strike was called.

On Wednesday, January 29, 1919, a committee approached Lord Provost James Stewart to intervene with the Government in favour of a forty-hour week. He agreed, and asked us to come back on Friday, the 31st.

We came, and thousands came with us. George Square was black with men.

Neil MacLean, Harry Hopkins, then District Secretary of the A.S.E., Emanuel Shinwell and I went into the City Chambers to hear what reply the Lord Provost had received.

While we were waiting in the Library we heard a great shouting in the Square. Looking out of the window, I was horrified to see squads of police batoning the people.

I smashed the window, stepped out on the balcony and shouted to the police to hold their hand.

I might as well have shouted to a hurricane. We hammered on the Lord Provost's door. No reply.

" Our place is outside," I called, and ran downstairs. Emerging from the entrance door of the City Chambers, I saw William Gallacher coming in, his face streaming with blood. I saw the police using their batons mercilessly. I did not know that the Sheriff had read the Riot Act. Stones and bottles were flying through the air ; the crowds were surging this way and that, driven by policemen.

I ran out, with arms widespread, to appeal for restraint and order. Then I knew—no more. I had been struck with a baton from behind.

When I came to, I was lying in the quadrangle surrounded by police, one of whom was bandaging my wounds. News flies quickly.

My first thought was to ask John Muir to go to my wife to tell her I was all right. He went at once, but before he arrived my wife had already been told that I had been killed.

I was hardly awake when John Wheatley and John Stewart came to beg me to go on to the

THE AUTHOR BEING BATONED BY A POLICEMAN AT GLASGOW

This photograph, produced in court, saved David Kirkwood from prison.

balcony and tell the crowd to disperse and meet in Glasgow Green.

Borrowing a cap to hide my bandages, I did as they asked. The crowd gradually migrated to the Green.

That night there was plenty of trouble in Glasgow. Gangs of wild men took advantage of the occasion to wreak their will. They marched through the streets, smashed windows, looted shops, and turned the town into pandemonium. The next day Glasgow was in the control of the Military.

I was in jail with eight others.

Released a fortnight later on bail, we awaited a High Court trial. At last it began.

The charge against us was of great length. We were accused of " instigating and inciting large crowds of persons to form part of a riotous mob to be assembled in George Square, Glasgow, for the purpose of holding up the traffic, of over-awing and intimidating the police officers on duty there, and of forcibly taking possession of the Municipal Buildings." Then followed references to riotous mobs, to the great terror and alarm of the lieges, stealing bottles and throwing them, assaulting the Sheriff, snatching the Riot Act from his hand, and much more.

The prosecution called one hundred and nine witnesses, mostly constables. We had almost as many. It was a weary job, that trial. For eleven dreary days it dragged its heavy way. Every evening I returned to Glasgow and spoke at meetings.

Fortunately for me, newspaper photographers had photographs of me being batoned. These were produced and corroborated my evidence that I had been struck from the rear while my hands were spread out in an appeal for peace.

Emanuel Shinwell was sentenced to five months' imprisonment, William Gallacher to three months. The other ten of us were found " Not Guilty."

I was free again, and once again was out of a job.

It was now nearing October. John Wheatley was in the Town Council. The engineers invited me to stand as their candidate in Mile-end Ward. I accepted, and became a Town Councillor.

My time was now fully occupied. I had been elected a member of the National Administrative Council of the Independent Labour Party and I was secretary of the Scottish Women's Housing Committee. Through this position I became an amateur lawyer. Every morning I attended the court, where as many as two hundred applications for ejection warrants were made by house proprietors. By the good grace of Mr Sheriff Fyfe, I was allowed to appear at the bar and, as friend to the tenants, plead their cause.

CHAPTER XIV

The Amateur Lawyer

ONE of the most valuable items in the equipment and training of a lawyer is the power of detachment. To him a case is a ' case.' To deal with it properly he keeps himself free from emotion. He may know that behind the case is a human problem of poverty, sorrow, despair. He stands aloof from all that.

I was not trained to be a lawyer. I had not by nature the attitude of a lawyer. I was not concerned with legal principles. It was the human problem that appealed to me.

The Summary Ejectment Court of the Sheriffdom of Lanarkshire at Glasgow is a revelation of the appalling misery in which thousands have to live, and a standing challenge to the system of society which makes such human misery possible.

Here are decided as many as two hundred cases in one day, each one of which is a human tragedy. House-factors, finding their tenants behind with their rent and knowing that a judgment for payment is useless on account of the poverty of the tenant, apply in this Court for warrant to turn the tenant out of the house. I am not complaining against them. It is their business to look after the affairs of the proprietor and, when one tenant does not pay the rent, to regain possession of the house and let it to a tenant who will.

In the years 1919 and 1920 the number of people in Glasgow who could not pay rent and live had grown to enormous figures. The heavy industries were depressed. Unemployment was rife. Public assistance was not so well organized or so generous then as it is now. Consequently day after day the Summary Ejectment Court was crowded with men and women who, if the Sheriff gave judgment against them, would find themselves without a home. There was no one to state their case and, in almost every instance, there was no legal case to be stated.

It fell to me to say what could be said on behalf of the poor creatures. It was a dreadful experience. No sooner did I enter the Court than I was surrounded by a crowd of frantic men and women, clutching my arm, rattling out their pitiful stories all at once, so that I could understand none of them.

Robert Burns has drawn a picture of the factor in a rural community, a picture drawn from his own memories of the suffering of his father. He puts the description in the mouth of Cæsar, the dog of the genteel, talking to his friend Luath, the dog of the lowly :

> I've noticed, on our Laird's court-day,
> An' mony a time my heart's been wae,
> Poor tenant bodies, scant o' cash,
> How they maun thole a factor's snash ;
> He'll stamp and threaten, curse an' swear,
> He'll apprehend them, poind their gear ;

While they maun stan', wi' aspect humble,
An' hear it a', an' fear an' tremble !
I see how folk live that ha'e riches ;
But surely poor folk maun be wretches.

But no picture of rural poverty can compare
with the grimy, sordid, diseased hideousness of life
in a Glasgow slum, as it was in 1920. After all,
however poor the peasant may be, two steps from
his humble black house will take him into God's
pure, clean air. For the city slum-dweller there is
no such escape. Inside and outside, he lives in
conditions pestilential and revolting. And yet, as I
saw the faces of the anxious, hopeless folk in that
Court, I could trace strong handsome features in
the men and often see a Madonna picture framed in
a frayed and dirty shawl.

At last a door opens behind the Bench. Every
one stands as the usher shouts, " The Court ! " The
Judge, bewigged and begowned, enters, bows to the
Court and takes his seat. The Court looks at him
with awe. In his hands is their destiny. A word
from him and they are homeless, or another word
and they may shuffle back to their miserable room,
safe from the street, the sleet, and the deadly fog.

As the usher calls the cases, the factor's clerk
on one side leans over to the tenant on the other.
That is where I come in. An offer was made to
pay so much a week. Would he accept ? In most
cases he would. The bargain was made with full
intention that it would be kept. Let us hope it
was.

So long as the negotiations were continued, the
Judge sat looking on, saying nothing. Only when

12

negotiations broke down was the case referred to him for final decision.

There are scenes from those days etched so deep on my mind that I see them now as clearly as when they happened.

.   .   .   .

A man's name is called. A woman steps forward. A dark shawl is round her head against which her face seems as pallid as death. She was a bonnie lass once, and not so long ago either, but her summer is gone with all its roses, and now she struggles to exist. She is her husband's deputy. She tells how she paid rent regularly until her husband was locked out through an engineering dispute. I have to tell the story for her. The Judge turns to me and says :

" Why don't these men have sense ? If they can't get the big wages they used to get, they will at least get something and these women would not be here."

" My Lord, I don't want to argue with you, but just let me say this : The working classes since away before the Factory Acts have been trying, through their Trade Unions, to improve and protect their standard of life, and it's because that standard is being attacked that the men are out the now."

" But there has been an inquiry and the men have been proved to be in the wrong. Why don't they accept that ? "

" Oh, my Lord, fair do, fair do ! "

" That's quite fair. They'd all get started to-morrow if they had the sense to go back."

" My Lord, we of the working class are all the

victims of a vicious system. This woman's man, me myself, we're all suffering from it. Look at this crowd here to-day. This is in Glasgow, the second city of the British Empire. These are Scotsmen and Scotswomen—the race that defied the might o' Rome.

> " Scots wha ha'e wi' Wallace bled,
> Scots wham Bruce has often led.

There they sit, the sons and daughters of this proud land, waiting to be put out of their houses. It's the system, my Lord."

" Yes ; but meanwhile what's to be done ? "

I turn to the woman : " Can you pay six shillings a week ? " The woman agrees. " She'll pay six shillings a week."

" All right," says the Sheriff, and away she goes.

" Next case."

.   .   .   .

A man comes forward who says, with a strong American accent, that he had left this country for the United States twenty-two years ago.

Clerk : " A very bad case, my Lord. Been here six times."

Sheriff : " Why did you not stay in America ? We have enough of our own to keep."

" I came over in 1916 to fight."

The Judge looks staggered. I take my chance.

" My Lord, I would ask you to give this man another chance. I understand he's got a job now. The call went out to the ends of the earth that the Motherland was in danger. This man heard that call away over in America and he couldn't get here quick enough. You know yourself what they were promised. Were the promises kept? You know they were not. Are you going to turn this defender of his country out on to the street now? No, my Lord, you would not do it."

I whisper to the man : " Can you pay seven and six? " The man nods.

" My Lord, he'll pay seven and six. I'm sure that'll do? "

Sheriff (wearily) : " Yes. Seven and six."

.   .   .   .

As her name is called, a poor old woman, neatly dressed in faded black, hobbles, on a pair of crutches, slowly and painfully to the rail. Partially paralysed and obviously very weak, she can scarcely stand. Her hands tremble so much that she has difficulty in controlling her crutches.

The factor's man is firm for immediate eviction.

" I want the house," he says harshly.

The old woman clings to the rail and turns to me. Who could resist such an appeal?

" My Lord, this poor old woman you see here is a widow. She has only one son. She offers five shillings a week. Is it not a shame to bring an old woman like this here at all? Is it not, my Lord? "

" Why didn't your son come himself? " asks the Sheriff.

" He's just new got a job and he's afraid he might lose it."

The tears stream down the old woman's cheeks.

The Sheriff softens.

" Oh, yes, my Lord, he's a good lad, he'll pay."

" All right, all right, do your best."

.   .   .   .

A bright lad of about ten comes to the rail, weeping.

" Why are you here ? " asks the Sheriff.

The boy whispers three words to the Clerk.

The Clerk nods sympathetically.

" What is it ? " asks the Judge.

" There's been a death, my Lord."

With a quick, angry glance at the factor's clerk, and an impatient jerk of his head towards the door, the Sheriff motions the boy away.

Law or no law, Summary Ejectment Court though it be, he will not allow a dead body to be thrown on the street.

.   .   .   .

A woman carrying a young baby in a shawl is called forward—a bright baby that smiles to me and looks round the court-room.

" A bad case, my Lord, only paid three weeks since January," says the Clerk. " This is her third time here. I don't see what else you can do."

" What is your husband ? "

" He's a dock labourer, my Lord."

Here the factor's man breaks in.

" This woman has been let off twice already, and it's no use. We want the house."

" I'm afraid I'll have to grant decree in this case," says the Judge.

" My Lord, I would ask you—give her just one more chance. She'll do it this time. She'll pay five shillings a week."

" No, no, Mr Kirkwood. She said that before.
I must——"

" My Lord, will you not give her another chance
—just one more chance—before you put her out
on the street ? Will you not, my Lord ? "

" No, Mr Kirkwood, I cannot."

I stand back, beaten.

The Judge proceeds to pronounce decree. A
silence in the Court. A little crow from the baby
makes the Judge look up. The child is gazing
toward his Lordship, who has last spoken.

The Judge raises his head and glances at the baby.
The stern features relax, and with a hurried
gesture as one who, vowing, " I will ne'er consent—
consented."

" All right, all right," he says, with a wave of
dismissal ; " but see you pay it this time."

.   .   .   .

At the next call an old man comes unsteadily
forward. The hair on his head is thick, but a dull
grey. The contour of the cranium, the remarkably
high cheekbones, the forehead so low that the hair
almost meets the eyebrows, the acuteness of the
facial angle, all indicate the primitive type. He
lurches forward until he collides with the rail,
sways backward from the impact, and would fall if
he were not held up. With massive hands grasping
the rail he stands gazing with vacant eyes at the
Judge.

I turn the man round, look in his face, speak his
name and smile. But there is no answering gleam
of recognition—the same stolid, stunned gaze. I
turn to the Sheriff.

" I know this man, my Lord, though I'm sorry to say he doesn't remember me. I once wrocht beside him in Parkhead Forge, and a real decent man he was. It's a pitiful sight. Give him another chance, my Lord. I'll stand for him."

" All right, Mr Kirkwood."

The long list of cases is ended. The Court is clearing. The Judge beckons to me to speak to him. I go to the bench, and he says, " That was a very sad case, Mr Kirkwood. You might let me help a little," and he hands me a ten-shilling note.

.   .   .   .

So passes the cavalcade of poverty, stunted and stripped and starved, one by one throughout the whole day, until Judge and Court and amateur Tribune of the People feel the virtue has gone out of them and, limp and listless, they wander to their homes.

CHAPTER XV

The Town Council

THE experience in the Courts gave me a new idea of the manner in which the people of Glasgow were forced to live. I was from Parkhead, where conditions were bad. But Parkhead had nothing comparable with Glasgow's slums. I learnt to understand the passion which rang in the voices of some of my colleagues when they made speeches about the housing conditions of their city. It was not the groan of the victims. It was the challenge of men who had been reared in happy circumstances. The victims were inarticulate. The reformers became their champions. Perhaps the conditions bred the deliverers.

The Town Council had at that time a group of ardent and earnest men who were nicknamed ' slum-smashers.' Whenever a chance came, they pounced in with speeches on housing. James Stewart, a barber, quiet, penetrating, and singularly sure of his facts ; John Wheatley, logical, concise, whose sentences fell like a steam-hammer ; Rosslyn Mitchell, in whom the missionary spirit was hereditary and who was as much at home addressing a midday meeting of professional and business men as a crowd of the poorest in a district hall ; James Welsh, a thinker who spoke little and achieved much. A few years later the House of Commons heard them all and wondered. In ten years the campaign was moving like a prairie fire, consuming much old wood on its way and leaving the land ready for new towns. But in those earlier days costs were prohibitive, interest was 6 per cent., and the cry of the people was silenced by shouts of high rates. All these men were my friends and allies.

I had new friends also. As a member of the Executive of the National Administrative Council of the Independent Labour Party, I came to know intimately the Parliamentary leaders on whom I was to depend to redeem the people from their sorrows. What a magnificent group they were ! Ramsay MacDonald, dominant wherever he was, a terrific worker, our best platform asset ; Philip Snowden, whose brain was as keen as a surgeon's knife, and whose courage and gallantry were beyond praise ; Bruce Glazier, who dreamed so many dreams which he has seen become realities ; Robert Smillie, with so much power and such gentle modesty, the very heart of loyalty.

Just about this time he was the hero of the hour. In 1920 the Sankey Commission was sitting. Robert Smillie outshone even the eminent Counsel at their own business of cross-examination. With him and Ramsay MacDonald I attended a meeting of the Executive at Seer Green, near Beaconsfield, close to Jordans, where the Penns had built their Friends' Meeting-house, and where, beneath mounds of green turf, so many of them lay buried.

On an evening Ramsay MacDonald, who claimed to be an authority on that countryside, invited me and a delegate to go for a stroll. MacDonald's strolls were about ten miles long and taken at five miles an hour. They were amusing too, for when Ramsay MacDonald walks, he kicks every pebble he sees on the road. It was a wild wintry evening, clouds were scudding across the moon, and soon the rain fell. We were near a wood. We entered for shelter. I suggested returning. MacDonald said we could go home through the wood. We walked on for an hour. Then MacDonald stopped.

" Davie, I'm wandered," he said.

The rain was now lashing. On and on we walked, sodden and sad, hour after hour, until at one in the morning we emerged on a chalk marsh. Our friend collapsed. MacDonald and I had to carry him. At last we reached a road, bordered by high hedgerows. Through the darkness and the lashing rain we marched until at last we saw a light. We roused the occupiers of the house and they directed us to our hotel. We must have been walking in circles for five hours !

It is a testimony to the endurance of Ramsay MacDonald that the adventure disturbed him not at all. I was exhausted, but recovered quickly. Our friend had caught a chill which he never quite threw off.

During 1921 the housing conditions in Glasgow became more and more acute. Thousands of soldiers had returned from active service to find high rents and no work. The Town Council grew weary of the perpetual pressure of the womenfolk for Government intervention.

One day a deputation from the Scottish Women's Housing Association attended at the City Chambers asking to be heard by the Council. The Council refused. It seemed to me to be a callous decision.

I marched out to the lobby and invited the women to come in. They trooped in. The Moderate members trooped out. The Lord Provost left the Chair. Sir John Lindsay, the Town Clerk, left his desk.

Thereupon John Wheatley took the Provost's Chair and called upon the deputation to address the Council. " The remanent members," as Sir John used to say, listened with attention.

By this time the Moderates had returned ' to see the fun,' so I had the pleasure of leading the deputation back to the lobby through an avenue of Moderates ! Not a word was spoken !

CHAPTER XVI

Westminster

MEANWHILE the nation was preparing for another General Election. The great Lloyd George, who, a few years before, was dictator of Britain, was losing his authority. The Kaiser remained unhanged. The golden dream of £22,000,000,000 with which he had juggled as Cinquevalli juggled with billiard-balls had remained only a dream. Britain had not handled the cash. Everything was going agley, as the " best-laid schemes o' mice and men " so often do. News that percolated through from Russia, Smyrna, and Ireland made the people shudder. Were we to begin another war against Turkey while we were flooding Ireland with " Black and Tans " ?

The Conservatives were the first to rebel. They had grown tired of the partnership and resolved to resume business on their own account. The Coalition collapsed. Mr Lloyd George resigned. Mr Andrew Bonar Law was called to form a Government.

We Glasgow Socialist candidates were well prepared for an election. For months, eleven of us had met every Saturday evening to discuss a plan of campaign. We did not fritter away our time mouthing toothless generalities. We were direct. Each evening we discussed a different subject, always from the point of view that we were to be the next Government. We began with a big " If."

" If we are in power, what are we going to do with the problem of Ireland ? "

" If we are in power, what are we going to do with the problem of the mines ? "

The result of this intensive method of discussion, led always by one of our number who had been chosen the week before to get up the subject, was that any one of us could go on to the platform of any other and speak without the risk of uttering conflicting views.

We had all been adopted for seats in and around Glasgow. Then Glasgow became the centre of the struggle. Mr Lloyd George and his faithful henchman, Lord Birkenhead, were coming to Glasgow ; Mr Asquith was coming to Glasgow. Mr Bonar Law, the Prime Minister, sat for the Central Division of Glasgow.

At one of our meetings we faced the fact that we were all contesting artisan constituencies and had no one to put up our case in the Central Division, the very citadel of the new Government. We decided that the Central must be fought. We knew that the man to fight it was one of our team, attending our meetings and having nursed a constituency for four years. John Wheatley and I were secretly instructed to ask him to put up against Bonar Law. There was no organization. There was no money.

We approached Rosslyn Mitchell without much hope. We told him what the team would like him to do and why.

" Then I'll do it," he said.

That election will be long remembered. The largest halls in the city were packed at seven, emptied at eight-thirty, and packed again at nine. He announced midday meetings for business men in the Merchants' House. They too were packed. Discarding chairman, introductions, and votes of thanks, he walked on to the platform and explained the futility of indemnities and reparations to men who had counted on millions. He advocated the Capital Levy at City Business Clubs, Rotary Clubs, and even from the rostrum of the Stock Exchange.

From the outside circumference of the city to its very heart, Glasgow was ringing with the message of Socialism. Within a week of the election day, it seemed likely that the whole team of eleven would win, that Bonar Law would be defeated, and that Socialism would be triumphant. Such energy, enthusiasm, and earnestness had not been known in Glasgow for generations. There we were, men who a few years before had been scorned, some of us in jail and many more of us very near it, now being the men to whom the people pinned their faith.

When, at last, the results were announced, every member of the team was elected—except our champion of the Central Division. What a troop we were ! John Wheatley, cool and calculating and fearless ; James Maxton, whose wooing speaking and utter selflessness made people regard him as a saint and martyr ; wee Jimmie Stewart, so small, so sober, and yet so determined ; Neil MacLean, full of fire without fury ; Thomas Johnston, with a head as full of facts as an egg's full o' meat ; George Hardie, engineer and chemist and brother of Keir Hardie ; George Buchanan, patternmaker, who knew the human side of poverty better than any of us ; James Welsh, miner and poet from Coatbridge ; John W. Muir, an heroic and gallant gentleman ; and old Bob Smillie, returned for an English constituency though he was born in Ireland and reared in Scotland.

Not since the days of the Chartists had any group of men so fully captured the imagination of the people as our team, and never had any group of men gone to the House of Commons with higher resolve than the Clyde Brigade of 1922.

We were full of revolt, but we were also full of hope. We were not boastful, but we were determined. " There's not a lum hat amongst us," said Bob Smillie. We did not belong to the " lum hat brigade." To be quite truthful, we knew little of the type of people whom we talked of as the " lum hat brigade." We were more of the kind celebrated in the old Scots song : " A lum hat wantin' a croon."

We were going to do big things. The people believed that. We believed that. At our onslaught, the grinding poverty which existed in the midst of plenty was to be wiped out. We were going to scare away the grim spectre of unemployment which stands grinning behind the chair of every artisan. We believed it could be done. We believed that this people, this British folk, could and were willing to make friends with all other peoples. We were ready to abandon all indemnities and all reparations, to remove all harassing restrictions imposed by the Peace Treaties. We were all Puritans. We were all abstainers. Most of us did not smoke. We were the stuff of which reform is made.

So serious were we of our responsibilities that, instead of holding a great Victory Meeting and making flamboyant speeches, we held a Service of Dedication, something on the lines of the Friends.

To the five thousand who attended the meetings we gave a copy of our Declaration, which Sir George Adam Smith, the Principal of Aberdeen University, referred to in the *Glasgow Herald* as " breathing the noble spirit of the Covenant." After singing the 124th Psalm, Scotland's Psalm of Deliverance, the Declaration was read clause by clause.

Here it is. This is what was in the hearts of the men o' the Clyde in their hour of triumph, when about to leave for Westminster as part of the 142 Labour Members of Parliament :

The Labour Members of Parliament for the City of Glasgow and the West of Scotland, inspired by zeal for the welfare of humanity and the prosperity of all peoples and strengthened by the trust reposed in them by their fellow-citizens, have resolved to dedicate themselves to the reconciliation and unity of the nations of the world and the development and happiness of the people of these islands.

They record their infinite gratitude to the pioneer minds who have opened up the path for the freedom of the people.

They send to all peoples a message of good-will, and to the sister nations of the British Commonwealth fraternal greetings.

They will not forget those who suffered in the War, and will see that the widows and orphans shall be cherished by the nation.

They will urge without ceasing the need for houses suitable to enshrine the spirit of home.

They will bear in their hearts the sorrows of the aged, the widowed mother, and the poor, that their lives shall not be without comfort.

They will endeavour to purge industry of the curse of unhealthy workshops, restore wages to the level of adequate maintenance, and eradicate the corrupting effects of monopoly and avarice.

They will press for the provision of useful employment or reasonable maintenance.

They will have regard for the weak and those stricken by disease, for those who have fallen in the struggle of life and those who are in prison.

To this end they will endeavour to adjust the finances of the nation that the burden of public debt may be relieved and the maintenance of national administration be borne by those best able to bear it.

In all things they will abjure vanity and self-aggrandizement, recognizing that they are the honoured servants of the people, and that their only righteous purpose is to promote the welfare of their fellow-citizens and the well-being of mankind.

Alas, that we were able to do so little !

We did our best. The actual results were meagre. But I sometimes think that the advanced guard of politics has for its chief purpose the work of making people accustomed to new ideas. If, by reasoning, by propaganda, by activity, we can change our opponents from rejoicing at the idea of destroying a proposal, into regret that they must destroy it, we are not far from making them glad to support it. Is not that the story of almost all the great redemptive movements of mankind? The dreamer, the rebel, the heretic, finds stoning, the bullet, or the stake. And, afterwards, the people rear a monument to his memory. He offers the people bread, which they scorn. Later they give him a stone in his honour.

Two days before the opening of Parliament we ten marched to the station in Glasgow *en route* for London. We marched through thousands of exuberant citizens. We were exuberant. I was the most exuberant of all. I was a smasher. By temperament I was an idol-breaker. The experience through which I had passed had made me a breaker not only of idols, but of those whose gods were idols.

No sooner had we arrived in London than we were plunged into the atmosphere of intrigue. We did not know that atmosphere. Plain, blunt, outspoken men we were. Not always right, but, thinking ourselves right, we had directness and definiteness. Now we breathed a new air, the air of intrigue, of personal vanity, of desire for position and power, of suggestion, of shrugged shoulders that often conveyed more than words.

The problem that was uppermost in the minds of the people we met was not what we were to achieve, but who was to be our leader. We had no doubt. We were Ramsay MacDonald's men.

It was the Clyde Group of Labour Members who made Ramsay MacDonald leader of the Party, and so opened the path to all his future greatness —and failure.

Our first meeting was with the I.L.P. members in the I.L.P. offices. To our great surprise, the I.L.P. members were not enthusiastically unanimous. The Clyde Group were. We proposed that the I.L.P. should nominate Ramsay MacDonald at the meeting of the Parliamentary Labour Party. The proposal was carried by our votes.

It was soon clear to us that the decision was not acceptable to the Trade Union members. The man whom we looked upon as the inevitable Leader was regarded with distrust by the older members of the Party. He seemed to move in a cloud of suspicion and distrust.

Arthur Henderson, " Uncle Arthur," said to me :

" You Clyde men are determined to put MacDonald in. Well, if you do, it will be only a few years before you will be trying to put him out."

I could understand Arthur Henderson, who had been so ardently pro-War when MacDonald was anti-War, but it was difficult to understand men who had been of MacDonald's way of thinking during the War feeling so antagonistic as they were.

So all-pervading was this feeling that even John Wheatley, whose admiration of MacDonald was unbounded, began to grow uneasy as to what was behind all the head-shaking and shoulder-shrugging.

"What does it mean?" he asked. "Is it jealousy? Can there be in their minds some knowledge that makes them uncertain?"

"I ken naethin' aboot it," I said.

"But," he went on, "the man seems to have no friends."

He was uneasy.

In my make-up there is no subtlety. To me MacDonald was the only possible leader.

Then he sprang a bomb. He let it be known that he was not going forward to election as leader. There was rumour that he did not feel well enough. We dismissed that easily. From the first day we had met, he had mentioned health. He was always tired. But we knew that he was a terrific worker.

At last we reached the full meeting of the Parliamentary Labour Party. MacDonald's men sat on the right-hand side of the room.

A wag said: "The MacDonalds are aye on the right wing—except at Culloden."

On the left-hand side sat the men who supported the Right Hon. John Clynes, who was Secretary of the General Workers' Union and had been pro-War, Food Controller in 1918, and Chairman of the Labour Party in the House of Commons in 1921–22. With him were the Trade Union Members. It was the first real trial of strength between the two sections, the political and the Trade Union.

Their chosen candidates were both of lowly

origin. Ramsay MacDonald was the son of a Lossiemouth farm-servant. He started as a pupil teacher, had come to London and earned a scanty living with the Cyclists' Touring Club, later as Secretary of the Scottish Home Rule Association, and thereafter as a journalist. He had been Secretary of the Labour Party from 1900 to 1912, and Chairman from 1912 to 1914.

John Clynes was a poor boy in Oldham who started work in a cotton factory and entered Parliament in 1906. For his services during the War he had been made a Privy Councillor and had been honoured by the Universities of Durham and Oxford, both of which conferred upon him the degree of D.C.L.

Nature had dealt unevenly with them. She had endowed MacDonald with a magnificent presence, a full resonant voice, and a splendid dignity. Clynes was small, unassuming, of uneven features, and voice without colour.

There they sat : Clynes at ease and indifferent ; MacDonald with his head in his hands, looking drawn, anxious, and ill.

When the votes were counted, MacDonald was elected by a narrow majority. The Clyde men had supported him solidly. His majority was less than the number of their votes. The result acted like magic on MacDonald. He sat up at once. All the lassitude and illness disappeared. He was as vigorous as any man in the room. John Wheatley looked at me and shrugged his shoulders. His uneasiness was growing. Clynes turned never a hair.

That evening we were to have a great demonstration of welcome to the new leader in Kingsway Hall. MacDonald did not appear. Clynes gallantly took his place and made a magnificent speech, ringing with loyalty and unity. That night he rose very high in our estimation.

When the House met, Labour had become for the first time His Majesty's Opposition, and Ramsay MacDonald the Leader of the Opposition.

CHAPTER XVII

Big Men

THE State Opening of Parliament is one of London's finest shows. When I saw it for the first time, I seemed to hear my father's voice quoting from his favourite poem :

> The boast of heraldry, the pomp of pow'r
> And all that beauty, all that wealth e'er gave.

It was there. In the streets the antique Royal coach, the glittering cavalry, flashing swords, and waving plumes. Within the House of Lords peeresses in every form of delicate fabric and peers glowing in red robe and ermine.

We talk of women being dressed. They are not in it with men ! For colour, splendour, and all the extras of ribbon and metal, men are supreme.

I am looking backward. The first time I saw it, it aroused in my heart neither respect nor awe. This was the panoply of a world that I hated and despised. I knew nothing of that world. To the artisan of an industrial area, the world of the rich and potent is unknown. He may have glimpses of it in the cinema, but it is more the Smart Set than Society. He may read of it in newspaper paragraphs, called Society Gossip, but it makes him sick. It seems so artificial, even tawdry. If he is engaged in political life on the Labour side, he regards that world as his enemy.

Benjamin Disraeli referred to Society and the People as two nations. In his day, more than in mine, there was an East and West, and it seemed as if never the twain would meet. In my time they had met, but it was the meeting of enemies.

I knew little of the Great Ones, the Powerful Ones, the Lordly Ones. Some men I knew have since been elevated to that select circle. When I knew them, they were still outside it. To me they were great men—Ramsay MacDonald, Philip Snowden, J. H. Thomas, Robert Smillie. They were my friends. We seldom think of our friends as among the Great Ones. At a distance a man looms big who, at close quarters, is no more than life-size.

I had met Mr Lloyd George in the atmosphere of hostility. I had met Mr Winston Churchill in an atmosphere of challenge. The others I did not know at all, but they represented all the things against which I had been fighting.

My antagonism was deep-seated. As far as my nature is capable of hate, I hated them all. There was nothing personal about it. I did not stop to examine any personal questions. They represented an authority against which I was in revolt. They had tried to crush me. They had failed. They and the world they represented were crushing my fellows down into poverty, misery, despair, and death.

When in 1922 I walked with John Wheatley from the House of Commons to the House of Lords

I saw the personification of all that world which I scorned.

Turning to John Wheatley, I said aloud: " John, we'll soon change all this."

The effect was like H. M. Bateman's famous cartoon of the soldier who dropped his rifle on parade. Such an expression was regarded as an explosion of sheer vulgarity. It was considered an outrage on the decorum of Parliament. And so it was. From my point of view, however, it was an explosion of indignation, an outburst of emotionalism, with a touch of exhibitionism and a spice of vanity.

I recognized this later in the day when my friend James Welsh, the Member for Coatbridge and Airdrie, a coal-miner and a poet, a man of fine feeling and high character, made his maiden speech. In words of real beauty and tenderness he described the scene of which we had both been witnesses. There was a frank admiration for the colour, the pageantry, the fine look of the men, and the loveliness of the women. Instead of scoffing at them he admired them, and from that standpoint he described the people of the coalfields and the iron belt. It was the finest maiden speech I have ever heard. It took the House of Commons by storm. It won admiration and friendship.

So it happened that two sons of the people went to Westminster. One was accepted as an orator of fine thoughts, the other as a rather vulgar interrupter.

It was a strange House. To me it was full of wonder. I had to shake myself occasionally as I found myself moving about and talking with men whose names were household words. More strange was it to find them all so simple and unaffected and friendly. In the House of Commons there is no snobbery except among the third-raters.

Mr Bonar Law was Prime Minister. He was one of the greatest men ever I met, very able and very sincere. He was a true House of Commons man. On one occasion we were in a hot debate. I sat for seven hours without leaving my seat. Bonar Law was there all the time. He was looking ill and languid. Then he rose to reply. Without a note, he took up and answered seven speeches in detail. I could not believe my ears and eyes. He spoke as if he had the speeches in front of him.

A week later we interrupted business for two hours with a constant barracking : " What are you going to do about unemployment ? " It was a violent attack. We won some concessions. Bonar Law showed no resentment. He remained calm and unruffled. Afterwards we happened to meet face to face in the Lobby. He stopped and said : " You Clyde boys were pretty hard on me to-day. But it's fine to hear your Glasgow accent. It's like a sniff of the air of Scotland in the musty atmosphere of this place."

What could a man do in the face of such a greeting ?

I had often been warned by my Socialist friends against the ' air ' of the House of Commons, its friendliness, its tolerance, and its freedom from rancour. I found that the warning was necessary.

One day after I had had a row in the House,

old T. P. O'Connor, the " Father of the House," came up to me and said :

" Don't do that sort of thing ! I've been through it. It does no good. You might as well stick pins in a crocodile. These people have a code. They will listen to argument, but abuse does not interest them."

Very early in my career I found how true that was. The ' conventions ' of the Commons are strong to bind. At first I thought they were nothing more than surface politeness. They are not. They are the foundation of the Parliamentary system. I have offended against these conventions very often. I am rough in speech and have never learnt the art of choosing my words or modifying my ideas. Sometimes I have been rebuked. I cared little for that. But rebuke is for the floor of the House. Outside in the Lobby it is not rebuke that rebukes. There is a courtesy and intimacy among Members which I learnt to understand after many strange incidents.

One of my lessons came from Mr Stanley Baldwin.

I had not met him, but I had glowered at him across the floor of the House. One day we started a scheme to hold up the debate. We were determined to make a protest, and chose the method of an all-night sitting.

A man's first all-night sitting is a fever, the second is a frolic, and the third is a farce. But it is a recognized means of protest.

On this occasion we carried on until seven in the morning. Mr Baldwin then moved the closure. We were furious. I shouted at him : " Man, vain man, drest in a little brief authority. You think you are a giant. You are nothing but a Uriah Heep."

I have seldom seen a man so taken aback. Then I remembered that Uriah Heep, whom we think of only as an example of false humility, was also a swindler. But, in the heat of the debate, I thought no more of it.

When we came out into the Members' Lobby I was astonished to see Mr Baldwin coming over to me. He said : " Mr Kirkwood, do you really think I am a Uriah Heep ? Have I appeared like that to you ? "

I had no arrow in my quiver to shoot at that. He had pierced a link in my armour that had never been pierced before. It was so unexpected that I had no protection against such an approach. I said at once : " No, you have not." " Then why did you say it ? It will be in *Hansard*, you know."

I put up a defence by saying that I had been enraged, and he said, laughing : " You will get much more than the closure to enrage you before you have been long in the House." I could say nothing more.

It was not that he made me feel ashamed, but he seemed such a big man who could take an insult like that. I have never had any reason to change the opinion I formed that morning. He is a big man, as sincere in his point of view as I am in mine.

Soon I had another surprise. I was standing in the Members' Lobby when Mr Winston Churchill came out of the House. He stopped and we shook hands. My mind flew back over six years to the day when I challenged him in the Ministry of Munitions to put me back into Beardmore's Works whether Beardmore wanted me or not. And there we were, both M.P.s, shaking hands in the Members' Lobby.

" I'm looking forward to you making the sparks fly here, Davie," he said. " And don't forget that I was the man who gave you the chance to make a name for yourself."

" That's true enough," I answered. " I remember it fine."

While we were talking, other Members gathered near us. He introduced me to some of them, calling me " David Kirkwood of the Clyde." Then in his own vivid and picturesque language he began to tell the group of our famous interview.

He is a great actor. He mimicked me in the flush of indignation and quoted some of the things I had said. He had every one laughing as he stood back, spread his arms wide, and imitated my challenge.

Then in a second he became the historian. He turned to them all and said : " The Clyde men never demanded very much. What they needed was some one who could understand their point of view."

Well, he was the man, and under his administration peace reigned supreme.

I had another object-lesson from Mr Lloyd George. Because he had been my worst oppressor I quickly found a chance to challenge him. In an

early stage of a debate I told the House that I
would make a violent attack on him later. What
was my surprise to receive a note saying how sorry
he was that, owing to an engagement which he
could not forego, he would be unable to be in his
place to hear my speech. He finished with an
apology.

That struck me as a queer thing for a man to do :
to write to another who had intimated that he was
going to attack him, apologizing for not being there
when he was to be attacked !

I had a ' go ' with Mr Neville Chamberlain.
He was talking about housing, and referred to
" courting in the parlour." Something roused me,
and I went my mile. He ignored the attack, but
five days later, when we met, he asked me what he
had said to hurt me, and went into a detailed
explanation of his housing ideas. I had meant to
hurt him, but he was concerned about what had
hurt me.

On another occasion I made a flaming speech
about some crofters in the Hebrides, and drew a
picture of their poverty and their struggle for land.
The vote was over. I lost. One of my opponents
met me in the Lobby and said : " I couldn't vote
for you, but I should like to help those men if I
may." He gave me a five-pound note.

This atmosphere of good-nature among Members
does not in any way affect their attitude in the
House itself. There, a man is expected to argue
his point with strength and conviction. If he is
sincere, he will be heard. If he is insincere or
artificial, there will be such a coming and going,

such a rustle of papers, and so many points of order that he can make no headway.

The House of Commons is the most tolerant place in the world ; but it will not tolerate insincerity.

Our Clyde Group had nothing to complain of in the treatment they received from the House. We were regarded as oddities and entertainers. We had a wonderful Press. The publicity which is the life-blood of the politician was ours in abundance. But soon the House recognized that we had a definite point of view, and they heard us gladly.

Most of all, they liked James Maxton. He was the hardest hitter of us all, but his blows were always according to the rules of the ring.

But James Maxton must have a chapter to himself.

CHAPTER XVIII

James Maxton, M.A., M.P.

FROM time to time there comes into the world a man who is different from other men.

It matters little in what circumstances he is born. He may be one of a large family, brought up in the same home, educated at the same school, and yet be as different from his brothers and sisters as he is from other men and women.

James Maxton is one of the different men.

He is so unlike other men that we have no one with whom we may compare him.

His standard of judgment is different. His standard of values is different. The things that entice and encourage other men to activity have no allurement for him.

Money? He seems never to think in terms of money, and certainly never allows it to weigh in the balance.

While he was Chairman of the I.L.P. a London weekly journal offered him a large sum to write an article. He said he would do it on two conditions—that he should choose the subject and the journal would take a full cover page of the *Labour Leader* for an advertisement at full advertising rates.

The editor asked how much. James Maxton

mentioned a figure. It was only half what the editor had decided to offer for the article. Jimmie wrote an article on " Porridge." The editor thought Jimmie was daft.

Quite a lot of people have thought him daft, because he does not conform to the general standard.

Popularity? He is the most popular man in the House of Commons and one of the most popular men in the land. He is sure of a full house whenever he speaks.

He is called " Jimmie " by friend and opponent alike.

In the days when he was a member of the Labour Party, even the insatiable love of speaking by the Trade Union representatives could not exclude him.

If a big show was on and he was asked to speak, he would say : " All right." Then there was much deliberation as to where he was to come in. " Oh, anywhere," he would say. " Put me anywhere you like, last if you like."

It is said that every politician covets the fruits of office. It is the guinea's stamp. Maxton cares nothing for the guinea's stamp—only for the gowd of sense and worth.

He is still talked of as a wild man. I remember the first time I saw him. It was in Camlachie, a district in the east of Glasgow, during the War. He was not well known. Neither was I, but I was asked to be chairman.

He was the nearest approach to a gipsy I had ever seen, a dark, swarthy, wire-rope gipsy. His

14

voice was strange, deep-toned, and resonant. His gestures were strange. His crouching attitude, the long sweep of his thin long arm and the stretch of his finger fascinated me.

But his speech !

I thought it wild and regardless. He threw discretion to the winds of heaven. I was not particularly discreet myself, but Maxton shocked me.

That evening we became friends. He treated me as if we had been comrades for years, a real happy-go-lucky Jim. It was just a sample of his genius for friendship.

Later, I went with him to Germany and Austria and Hungary. He knew little French, and less German. I was astonished, for I thought a Master of Arts knew all languages.

But he made friends everywhere.

On the Rhine we met a black Algerian soldier of the French army of occupation. James talked to him like a vera brither, and was so sympathetic with him in his longing to return to his native country that when we said " Good-bye " the Algerian was on the verge of weeping.

Only once I saw him angry. Like most gentle people, he was terrific in anger.

At a Belgian port our two handbags were snatched from us by a French-looking porter and carried to the train—a trifling walk. Maxton gave him a florin. The man grumbled, and was loath to give up our bags.

Maxton opened out in a dozen perorations of scorn that would blister a regiment. The man

J.M...."For I am a Pirate King."

ALL : " YOU ARE !
OUR JIMMY'S A PIRATE KING ! "
(*Pirates of Penzance*)

LABOUR NIGHTS ENTERTAINMENTS.

Cartoon by Low, reproduced by kind permission of the "Evening Standard"

gasped. When he recovered his breath he said :
" You're just two dam' Scotchmen."

" Ay, an' a kent whaur ye cam' frae," said
Maxton, with his favourite platform crouch.

The sham Frenchman fled, followed by our
laughter, which was neither low nor sweet.

We raced home from Berlin for the election of
1922.

All Parliament thought Maxton a wild man.
The House of Commons waited for his maiden
speech. When he rose they expected fireworks,
squibs, rockets, and crackers. They saw the coke
fire glow before a watchman's hut.

The firebrand disappointed them.

His power over the House was a slow and
steady growth. He carved his own niche. He
had to carve it himself, for there was no niche that
could hold him. And the tool he used was
sincerity.

To serve the working-class was his aim, and he
served them by the directness of his speech, the
clearness of his ideas, and the glow of a kindly,
genial, tender, and considerate nature.

How considerate he is ! When I was arrested
after the Riot of the Forty Hours' Strike, I was
taken from the Central Police Station to Duke
Street Jail in a Black Maria. Maxton was waiting
outside the Central. As I passed he put something
in my hand. It was a clean white handkerchief.

He had remembered my great weakness for a
clean hankey.

It was because of my deportation that he
served twelve months in Calton Jail.

On the Sunday after the deportation he addressed a crowd on Glasgow Green, and told them they were not worth a docken if they went back to work before we were returned to our homes. He was arrested.

Then we had the queer paradox, that he was in jail and I was free.

James Maxton is the product of his times, but he would have become notable in any circumstances.

He is that rare combination of fearless oratory and absolute truth. He has never been pulled up for an inaccurate statement. He is a great speaker.

Sometimes he is more than that. He is a prophet.

He looks and speaks and acts like a man inspired. He loses himself, though he never loses his temper. At such times he speaks with tongue of fire, as no other man I have ever heard in the House.

Why then is he, with all the equipment of a leader of men, still a wanderer in the wilderness ?

Baldwin, Churchill, Elliot, Simon, Lloyd George, and Samuel all recognize his power. The Labour Members know it. They cheer, but they do not follow.

They fear him.

He is often so abstract and so dreamful that the Trade Union members are afraid lest he lead them in paths where they do not care to tread.

It is not as if he was destructive. He attacks not persons, but arguments. Bubbling over with humour, he can pour delicious ridicule upon an argument. He can denounce. He can wither with scorn.

But he never leaves a vacuum. He is by nature affirmative.

He has his message. It is the same message always. He is a real Tribune of the People. He believes in them. He loves them. He beckons to them to go with him. If they go, he is good company. But if they do not go he will walk alone.

It is the destiny of some men to tread the road that is uphill all the way and to tread it alone.

In after years men mark the footprints where they trod, and show them to their children.

Then they become legends.

CHAPTER XIX

The Clyde Group

NEXT to James Maxton, I think I was the favourite of the paragraphists. I had not James Maxton's skill in speaking. Mine was a coarser method, and my speech was rough. Often, when I was most in earnest, the House laughed at me. The Members were very friendly, only they treated me as if I was a very raw young man.

The biggest reputation among our group was made by John Wheatley. The Members disliked him, but they respected him. His arguments were cold and challenging. Sometimes he sneered. That was unforgivable. It is the least effective form of speech in the House. James Maxton never sneered.

The result was that James Maxton was treated as a friend who had cranky ideas. John Wheatley was considered an outsider. Two incidents will show the difference and one of them was a deep lesson to John Wheatley.

James Maxton, who always looked so ill that, when he *was* ill, it was not noticed, crumpled up. He had to undergo a serious operation. Just afterwards, Winston Churchill invited me to his room. His brother John was there. He introduced

me as " one of the two mildest men who ever slit
a throat." Then he asked if I had news of
" Jimmy Maxton." I told him the operation was
over and had been successful. He handed me the
two volumes of his *Life of Lord Randolph Churchill*,
and asked me to give them " as a token of my
friendship for James."

The other incident concerns John Wheatley.
It is part of the stock-in-trade of ruffling politics to
fling out a challenge to an opponent to debate a
subject in public. The idea behind the challenge
is that the speaker represents public opinion, as the
adversary would soon see if he would come and
state such views in public.

John Wheatley and Sir Robert Horne were in
conflict as to the views of the workers on a certain
point. There was a flat denial. John was ready.

" I challenge the right honourable gentleman to
come to Shettleston and debate with me in
public."

" I accept the challenge," replied Sir Robert.

That was a stunner. No one ever expects such
a challenge to be accepted. It is like the question
which speakers ask, knowing it will not be answered,
so that they may answer it themselves to their own
satisfaction—as if that clinched the argument.

What was to be done ? The challenge was
accepted. It was almost like taking an unfair
advantage of a man to accept his challenge. What
kind of a show should we have in Shettleston with
Sir Robert Horne, the lawyer, politician, business
man ? I was interested, because Shettleston is next
door to Parkhead. But why worry ? He may not

come after all. Many a man has accepted a challenge to a duel and then drawn out.

Not so this time. Sir Robert Horne came. He was suffering from a sore throat. It was sufficiently bad to have warranted a cancellation of the meeting. But he came and carried through the debate with much rapier cut-and-thrust, but with complete good humour. The audience thoroughly enjoyed the tussle.

When it was all over, John Wheatley said to me : " David, you remember me saying that the House of Commons, apart from party politics, breeds big men ? "

I said : " Ay, I mind fine."

" Well," he continued, " there's an example. These fellows are big enough to stoop to conquer. It is a lesson we have yet to learn."

The year of opposition increased Ramsay MacDonald's political stature immensely. He was the outstanding figure on the Opposition side. He and Philip Snowden were leading the official Opposition, but that position was subjected to perpetual challenge by the two wings of the Liberal Party and their leaders, Mr Asquith and Mr Lloyd George. Our men were harassed, and MacDonald was grossly overwrought. Besides leading the Party in the House, he was writing a stream of newspaper articles to earn a living. He did not receive the high fees which others could demand. He was always at the beck and call of his followers and his prospective followers, men in the House, and men hoping to be in the House. There was trouble in the Party itself.

John Wheatley and I had pinned our faith to Ramsay MacDonald. He was our leader. Although I was an earnest Trade Unionist and believed, as I believe now, in the great value of Trade Unionism, I found out very quickly in Parliament that a man was not necessarily a good Parliamentarian simply because he was a good Trade Unionist.

Sometimes, indeed, he was restricted in his political outlook by the fact that his chief interest was in his Union and his first loyalty was to his own section.

MacDonald and Snowden, aloof from sectional interests, always seemed to me to have a wider outlook on political affairs than the men who came into politics through industrial channels.

It was the same with Wheatley, Maxton, and Tom Johnston. There was no one behind them directing them how they were to act or expecting of them that they would act in a certain way. Besides, MacDonald and Snowden had devoted a lifetime to the building up of the Movement.

We were not a very happy family. The Left Wingers tried to push him on more quickly than it was his nature to go. I was a Left Winger. So were all the Clyde men. We felt that our leader, the man who had been elected by our votes (we never forgot that), was veering too much to the Right, growing too closely knit with the Trade Union section instead of the I.L.P. section. Snowden seemed to be going in that direction also.

But the greatest difficulty arose through the relationship between him and Philip Snowden.

They were hardly on speaking terms and sometimes for days would not even look at each other. They were so different from each other that they had no common ground on which to build friendship.

MacDonald was cloudy. Snowden was precise.

MacDonald roamed round a subject. Snowden went direct.

MacDonald was fond of the company and conventions of High Society. Snowden, notwithstanding his wife's eminence among "the great," despised the artificiality of it all.

It is amusing to me now to see Ramsay MacDonald still a commoner and Philip a viscount. Ten years ago I could have imagined Ramsay MacDonald an earl—but never Philip Snowden.

Ramsay MacDonald told me once that a certain nobleman had chaffed him about his association with our Movement and had added : " You know, you are really one of us." He was not displeased by the remark. He is of that mould.

But Philip was the Robespierre, the incorruptible democrat, untemptable by the lure of honours.

In 1922–23 the future was hidden from us. We believed in MacDonald and Snowden. We knew MacDonald's weaknesses, his sensitiveness to criticism, his love of the feeling of power, and his quite childlike vanity. But he had the knowledge, the perception, the earnestness, and the double accomplishment of doing big things with splendid style and little gracious things with charming frankness. Little Stephen Walsh, who was

Secretary of State for War in MacDonald's first Cabinet, and an authority on Shakespeare, said MacDonald was a Coriolanus without his courage.

In May 1923 Mr Bonar Law resigned. There was great talk as to his successor. The choice of Mr Baldwin surprised us. He was not very well known in the House. He soon became well known. Everybody learned to respect him, and among his opponents many came to regard him with a real affection. It was sometimes difficult to continue the attack just because of that.

He is the most democratic and tolerant man in the House of Commons. No matter what point of view is expressed, however advanced, he will treat it as a possible solution though he may disagree with it himself.

Some leaders win through by assurance that they are always right. Others win through on Cromwell's idea of thinking it possible that they may be wrong. That is largely the difference between the autocrat and the leader of democracy. Mr Baldwin is a leader of democracy.

Mr Stanley Baldwin had been Chancellor of the Exchequer, but had not introduced a Budget. It was evident that there would be a general election soon. It came very soon.

In January 1924 Labour was returned as the largest Party in the House. It had not a majority, and there was a good deal of doubt as to the wisest course to pursue. At our Party meetings most of us of the Left Wing were against assuming the responsibilities of office. We were overborne by a large majority.

As soon as it was certain that we were to be His Majesty's Government, the air became electrical. Ramsay MacDonald was now all-powerful. He had a free hand—and there were plenty who were ready to feed out of it. The lure of office, power, and emoluments was strong. The politician expects to occupy a position in a Government. Most politicians think themselves of Cabinet rank. There is nothing disgraceful in that. A man goes to Parliament because he is elected. The first concern of an M.P. is to keep his seat. Naturally he hopes to rise in the Party and in the Government.

The Clyde Group was not enamoured of being the Government. Nor were they personally intent on office. Soon, however, news percolated through that one had been offered a position. Then came gossip that others hoped to be offered. The surprise was John Wheatley. He had been a thorn in the side of Ramsay MacDonald. His early hero-worship had cooled. He was critical in the Party meetings and even in the House itself.

We heard that he had been offered an Under-Secretaryship and had refused. Well done, John! Then we heard that he had been offered a position in the Cabinet and had accepted. He became Minister of Health. He was a magnificent success as Minister of Health, but we felt that he had left us.

Robert Smillie was offered a Cabinet position and declined, on the ground that he had been a Trade Union official all his life, that being a Minister was a different business altogether, and that he was too old to learn a new trade. That was just like Bob Smillie. He had given his life to the cause, but he never thought of himself as a creditor of the Party.

The new Government was as strong as circumstances allowed. Circumstances did not allow it to be as strong as it might have been. So many men had claims, not on account of brain-power or suitability, but on account of services rendered to the Party either as Trade Union leaders or as propagandists. They demanded that the Party should acknowledge their services. Peculiarly enough, those whose services had been least conspicuous expected the highest rewards. Some, who had never stepped outside of the spheres in which they received payment for every service given, seemed to think that the Party was their own creation. Some of the Trade Union section felt that they should, as Trade Unionists, have a fair share of the responsibility, a more generous share than the new Prime Minister was prepared to grant. Ramsay MacDonald must have many merry memories of those days of Cabinet-making.

The Labour Government of 1924 lasted from January until October. It was a pitiful affair. The one big outside man was Lord Haldane. We suspected that he had had rather too much say in the formation of the Government. He was Ramsay MacDonald's favourite at the time. Ramsay MacDonald was in the habit of having one close friend. The friendships did not last very long, but they were very close while they lasted. Lord Haldane, then Mr Sidney Arnold (who became a peer), then Oswald Mosley, then Lord Thomson, then Lord Londonderry. It was the same with his colleagues. One by one they stepped into the inner circle and then stepped out again. He could not stand a rival near the throne. This has often been called vanity. It was self-reliance.

When I hear Ramsay MacDonald spoken of as stupid and conceited, I laugh. He is the most self-reliant man I ever knew. He was always like that —very, very sure of his own views. And, truth to tell, he was most often right. In the days of the I.L.P., he and Philip Snowden were often at loggerheads. Ramsay MacDonald took broad views and was far-sighted. Philip Snowden's views were precise, narrow, and moulded by the immediate circumstances. The Scotsmen used to call him ' nippet.' He argued about details, like a lawyer. Ramsay MacDonald argued on broad principles.

This temperamental antagonism was emphasized by personal dislike. They should have been divorced for incompatibility of temper. Instead, they continued their association for the sake of the family. They both regarded the Labour Party as their child. They had not given it birth, but they had fostered it and developed its strength. It was to them what Parkhead was to Beardmore.

MacDonald suffered from nerves. The Clyde Group irritated him. The directness, almost roughness of speech which is characteristic of Glasgow men of all shades of opinion, and which in former days he had admired so much, became less agreeable. He thought we were lacking in loyalty and in manners. He wanted a compact party, but we were in a hurry to fulfil our promises to the people and became critical of him and the Party.

The Government collapsed on a trifling incident that would not have affected a Prime Minister who had a greater control of his followers and a less sensitive disposition. To Ramsay MacDonald, the conduct of the Liberals was a personal humiliation, the one thought he could not tolerate.

If Ramsay MacDonald and Snowden had been friendly and had consulted together, the Labour Government would not have collapsed as it did. I am sure that Philip Snowden would not have published the absurd Zinovieff letter. What a laugh I had over that letter !

During the past five years the Bolshevik Government of the Russian Republics had been steadily consolidating its position. Counter-revolution, massacre, anarchy, famine, and pestilence had swept over the country. Red armies of the Bolsheviks, directed by Leon Trotsky, and White armies of Kornilov, Alexieff, Deniken, Wrangel, and Koltchak, aided by British, French, Italians, and Japanese, had reduced the land of Russia to desolation. At last the counter-revolutions were at an end. Their creators and followers were dead or had disappeared to eke out a living in the cities of Europe. The Red Terror was triumphant and the time had arrived when the new economics might be tested. There were many of the leaders of the Bolsheviks who believed that to make the Communist system a success there must be a world revolution. To them it seemed that there could not be a successful Communist *régime* in Russia while the rest of the world was existing in a capitalist society.

To this country the Bolshevik Government presented two fronts. On the one hand they asked us for a loan, in order to re-establish their industry. On the other hand, they were carrying on a propaganda with the idea of bringing about a revolution in Britain. Naturally, the Socialists in Parliament paid attention to the call for help, while to the Conservatives the paramount element was the ' pernicious propaganda.'

This emphasis, on both sides of the House rather lopsided, was a hidden fire which any wind might fan into flame. The wind was the proposal of the Government to grant to Russia a loan of £40,000,000. The arguments in its favour were sound enough. The loan was to be granted in goods, which would help to remove the burden of unemployment. The recovery of Russia was essential to our export trade and desirable because of our food supplies.

There was a condition attached to the loan— that seditious propaganda should cease.

The wind succeeded in turning the fire into a furnace. Much of the heat of it was blown in the direction of the Clyde Group. For some reason, which remains a mystery, the Conservatives of England looked upon the Clyde area as seething with Communism. Often I have heard Glasgow talked of as if its citizens were in a state of perpetual revolution. I have even known of an Englishman of education, whose wife was invited by an old

school-friend to visit her in Glasgow, forbidding her
to accept the invitation because he thought it was
dangerous. The whole idea is as much a myth as
the Russian soldiers who were supposed to have
landed in Caithness during the War. Every one
had a friend whose cousin had seen them with snow
still on their boots after a march of three days in
Scotland !

So strong was the antagonism to the Russian
Loan that it was used as an argument to prove that
the Socialist Government was Bolshevik.

The time was ripe to prove to the people of
Britain that the Bolsheviks were devils at heart.
As the general election moved on its exciting way,
rumour ran round that we were to expect a bombshell. It came in the form least expected.

Rumour had said that a London paper of large
circulation was going to publish a circular letter
which had been discovered, in which directions
were given to the British Communists for the
revolution in Britain. That is not what happened.
The letter did not appear as a newspaper stunt.
It appeared as an official document, and with it
was published an official Foreign Office protest,
stated in terms much stronger than the language of
diplomacy. Mr Ramsay MacDonald was Foreign
Secretary as well as Prime Minister. Nothing
could have been firmer evidence of the authenticity
of the document than this official protest. But no
such document existed. All that had been seen was
a copy of an alleged copy. On the face of it, the
document was a fake.

It was supposed to **have been** signed " Mac-

15

Manus." Here was my little Irish fellow-deportee, who had been scared out of his wits by the Zeppelin, become a person of such importance that he could make the nation quake at the mention of his name !

If Philip Snowden had been consulted, he would have seen the immediate effect of the Zinovieff letter and of the extraordinary schoolmaster-like reply by Ramsay MacDonald as Foreign Secretary. I suppose Ramsay MacDonald thought, with his long view :

" Here is the letter. The *Daily Mail* is going to publish it. I will publish it first with such a reply as will show the people of Britain that we, the Labour Government, have no truck with the Bolsheviks."

It did not work out that way. The people accepted the letter as genuine, just as Ramsay MacDonald had accepted it as genuine. The reply of Ramsay MacDonald only had the effect of making it seem more serious. If it had been printed by a newspaper, the people would have said : " Oh, this is a newspaper stunt." But when they saw that Ramsay MacDonald accepted it as genuine, they said : " Then why is he talking about a loan of £40,000,000 to Russia ? " To them there was something sinister about it all.

In my election speeches I never referred to the Zinovieff letter except to say it was a fraud. I could not be serious about a letter from Wee MacManus, especially when it was signed by the surname only —just " MacManus "—as if he was Lord Mac-manus. It was so ridiculous that I never heard it mentioned without feeling myself laugh, but it was a very serious element in the country. Posters appeared in which Socialist candidates were portrayed with long hair, bulging eyes, squat noses, bristling moustaches, and beards like kitchen scrubbing-brushes. It was a picture of a ' stage ' Cossack.

" It's no verra like ye, Davie," said the engineers of Clydebank, as if I had been showing them a family album.

CHAPTER XX

In Opposition

THE 1924 election was lost—partly because of the Zinovieff letter, which was a swindle, and partly because the Labour Government had accomplished nothing and had challenged nothing. If it had challenged and been beaten on a vote, we should have had a chance. But it had not been a 'regular royal queen,' only a 'half-and-half affair.'

Because we were neither fish, flesh, fowl, nor good red herring, the people voted for Stanley Baldwin and the roast beef of old England.

Mr Stanley Baldwin once said he became Prime Minister by accident. He soon showed that accident could make a good choice. He had a tremendous majority. For eighteen months his Government carried on against the combined opposition of Labour and Liberals. Having been defeated at the election and being overwhelmed in the House, the Trade Unions began to think of other means of obtaining their ends.

Coal, which has been the source of our material prosperity and at the same time the cause of much of our political distresses, became the dominant factor in the country. Seeing no hope in political measures, the coal-miners resolved to take industrial measures. The Trades Union Congress was behind them. We began to look forward to a General Strike. This was a new weapon in our country, but it had been tried on the Continent without much success. There must have been some inkling in the minds of Parliament that an attempt at a General Strike might be made.

In 1925 Mr Baldwin made one of his most

THE CONSERVATOCIALISTS.

Mr AUSTEN MAXTON.   Mr J RAMSAY BALDWIN.   Mr WINSTON KIRKWOOD.   SIR W. JOYNSON-LANSBURY

Cartoon by Low, reproduced by kind permission of the "Evening Standard"

famous speeches. It is known as the " Peace in our Time " speech. It has become a catch-word. It is really a classic. In 1925 the Conservatives were cock-a-hoop. They had the biggest majority in their history. A large group of them decided to introduce a Bill to change the basis of Trade Union contributions to the political fund. A member of a Trade Union could, by giving notice, contract out of the political fund. The Bill proposed that no member should pay to the political fund unless he contracted in. The Opposition was in angry mood.

Mr Fred Macquisten, K.C., moved the second reading, and Mr Greaves-Lord, K.C., seconded. They were heartily cheered by the Government benches. The House prepared for a good scrap. To the surprise of every one, Mr Baldwin moved an amendment, thereby challenging his own Party. He spoke very quietly. As he outlined his view of the development of industry into Employers' Federations and Employees' Trade Unions, the House was all attention. He began to talk of his own experiences in his works, where he knew not only every man on the ground, but the circumstances of his family. It was a picture of the old family business in which when, owing to a Coal Strike, the works were closed down, the men were maintained by Mr Baldwin himself. Then he warned in words that were prophetic :

" In this great problem of the clash of great combinations which is facing the country, it may be that in after years, from one side or the other, disaster may come."

He made a plea for greater understanding between the rival associations of masters and men ; without a partnership there would be a crash. He ended with the famous peroration :

" I know that there are many in all ranks and all Parties who will re-echo my prayer : ' Give peace in our time, O Lord.' "

When he said that, the Bill was dead. The House was completely won. All the bitterness and anger of my side of the House evaporated. The other side, which had cheered the mover and seconder, now cheered more fervently the executioner.

I said that the speech was prophetic. Within a year the clash came. The General Strike was a test of the power of Trade Unionism. " As these associations become more powerful there may come a time when they may directly injure the State." That was Mr Baldwin's prophecy. Twelve months later the State proved that it would resist such an injury.

The purpose of the General Strike was to obtain justice for the miners. The method was to hold the Government and the nation up to ransom. We hoped to prove that the nation could not get on without the workers. We believed that the people were behind us. We knew that the country had been stirred by our campaign on behalf of the miners.

Mr Arthur Cook, who talked from a platform like a Salvation Army preacher, had swept over the industrial districts like a hurricane. He was an agitator, pure and simple. He had no ideas about legislation or administration. He was a flame. Ramsay MacDonald called him a guttersnipe. That he certainly was not. He was utterly sincere, in deadly earnest, and burnt himself out in the agitation.

I was heartily in favour of the General Strike. I believed we should see such an uprising of the people that the Government would be forced to grant our demands. Ramsay MacDonald was in favour of it. Philip Snowden was in favour of it. J. H. Thomas was in favour of it. When it came, it was so tremendous that there was no one big enough to control it. It had no sooner started than the big men began overtures to bring it to an end. The fact is, it was a failure. As a demonstration of working-class loyalty, it was the greatest event of my time. Not only the artisans, who were accustomed to leave a job or be paid off at a moment's notice, but the organized blackcoat workers sacrificed their position, their livelihood, their superannuation funds, everything, to help the miners.

But it was very soon clear that the nation would not allow any section of the community to supersede Parliament.

Trained through centuries to regard Parliament as the instrument of redress, they disapproved of actions which seemed to reduce the stature of Parliament. The challenge to the nation was accepted by the nation with this distinction. The challenge was serious, but it was accepted in a spirit of fun.

A trifling inconvenience is resented because it usually only affects a few, but the dislocation caused by the General Strike was so universal that people laughed at each other's difficulties and their own. When I saw car-loads of girls driving through the streets of London looking upon the experience as if it were a picnic, I knew that we were beaten.

In a few days it was all over, and some of those who had encouraged it were writing newspaper articles denouncing it, as if they had been opposed to it all along. Others who had encouraged it ran away as soon as they saw its extent. It exhausted the funds of the Trade Unions. It shook the faith of many members in the wisdom of their leaders. It dislocated industry, and it increased the power of Parliament, which it had been formed to supersede.

The salvation of this country has to be worked out along constitutional lines. We can forge out our destiny on the anvil of the House of Commons. It is a slow process. In this country it is the only sure one.

I do not dictate to other peoples how they are to operate. That is their affair. But, for us, the House of Commons is the forum for speech and reasoning and the Government the machinery for action.

It seems to me that anything that belittles them will not be tolerated by our race.

Among other things, the General Strike provided a perfect example of the style of speech of Mr Winston Churchill, the Chancellor of the Exchequer. Most of the very great speeches I have heard have been spoken in very simple words. That is where Mr Winston Churchill differs from the others. His speeches are full of surprising phrases. I think he has the largest vocabulary of any man in the House and he is by far the most dramatic speaker.

He was never more dramatic than at the close of the General Strike of 1926. During the Strike he had been responsible for the publication of *The British Gazette*, a miserable little sheet of news that was the object of much ridicule. After the collapse of the General Strike a debate took place in the House. The Labour Party lashed Mr Churchill. It seemed a deliberate attempt to taunt him into fury. He did not disappoint his baiters. He took up their challenge in a heroic style of speech. In flashing phrases he denounced the wickedness and folly of the General Strike. Then he began to warn the Trade Union elements of what would happen if they did it again. The whole House waited for the momentous words. Would he threaten to declare a state of Civil War? Would he call out the Army in a civil dispute? Would he arrest the leaders? Very solemnly he proceeded with his warning: "If ever this and if ever that . . ." Then, working to his climax with the most awesome solemnity, he paused and said: "Then I will publish another *British Gazette*!" For a moment the House could not collect its wits. Then there came such a crash of laughter as I have never heard in the House. The Conservatives were in a frenzy of delight. Our boys could not resist the ridicule and joined in the laughter. That astonishing performance made another General Strike impossible. No one can be serious when the victims treat their victimizers as a joke.

The General Strike led me into trouble. Sir William Joynson-Hicks, always called "Jix," was Home Secretary, and upon him fell the chief burden of the strike. I liked "Jix." He was a character. He was no favourite with my colleagues. He had made a stupid blunder by instructing a raid on "Arcos," the headquarters in London of the commercial section of the Russian Government, for the purpose of discovering an imaginary document which wasn't there. But he was a gracious creature, rather like a character from Dickens, wearing a long frock-coat and a

stick-up collar and a four-in-hand tie. He was a
personage. He was also a Puritan.

During the General Strike I made a speech in
which I said that if my country treated my wife
and family as the miners were being treated I'd
" blow the whole thing to babarags."

He challenged me to repeat that speech outside
the House. I accepted the challenge, and repeated
it at Cloan, near Sheffield.

He came down on me like a ton of bricks. I
was summoned to the Court of Renishaw. A
policeman gave evidence of what I had said.

" Could you understand him ? " asked my
lawyer.

" Easy," said the constable.

I was called upon to speak to the Court, and
in my broadest accent I recited a few lines of a
ritual we used in the I.O.G.T. :

> . . . in naturre we find no strrong drrink, nothing
> thaat caan intoxicate. The Almighty and Allwise
> prreparred but one drrink, purre watterr. This
> He furrnished bounteefully and sent it courrsing
> thrrough the airrth, rrushing down the hillside,
> glancing in the sunbeam, bounding thrrough the
> valley, distilling in the dew and trreasured in the
> mighty deep. Placed at the head of all animate
> crreation, man is the only crreature that sinks below
> his level and yields to a strrange and acquirred
> appetite.

" What has Mr Kirkwood said ? " asked my
lawyer.

" I dunno," said the constable, " but at Cloan
it was English he spoke."

The Bench, very imposing County people, retired to consider their judgment, and then fined me £25. Half a dozen M.P.'s were in the Court, and Maxton, in the broadest Glasgow dialect, shouted :

" Et's no' fairr. It's no' bin a fairrr trrrial," whereupon he was summarily ejected.

CHAPTER XXI

The Dominion of Canada

THE year 1928 gave me one of the ' crowded hours of glorious life ' that come to very few of my class and only once to them. Since my entry to Parliament I had been a member of the Empire Parliamentary Association. It is all-British and spans the world. Whenever a statesman of any part of the British Commonwealth of Nations, a Governor of a Crown Colony, or a prominent public man of India came to London, a meeting of the Association was summoned. The visitor gave an address on his country and answered questions.

Those meetings I regarded as the most educative part of Parliamentary life. They were superb.

Every two years a delegation of all the British Parliaments makes a visit to one of the distant Dominions or Colonies. In 1928 the invitation came from the Dominion of Canada. The choice of members of the delegation is made by a small committee composed of the very highest men in Parliament.

To my surprise and gratification I was invited to submit my name to the Selection Committee. I did so and was chosen. Two of my personal friends were chosen also : Thomas Johnston, M.P. for West Stirlingshire, and Rosslyn Mitchell, who, having failed to defeat one Prime Minister in Central Glasgow, had defeated another in Paisley, and was known as " the Member for Paisley." He had become notable on account of his speeches in the House of Commons, especially those he delivered in the Prayer Book debate. The first of the two was the most moving occasion I have ever witnessed in the House. All the great speakers were on the lists that day. It was a real tournament of oratory. In these days of bread-and-butter politics there are few opportunities for great speaking. Besides, party lines are so finely drawn that votes are not affected by speeches. On this occasion, however, it was different. The issue was one which divided England vertically, not horizontally. Although every Member was ticked off on the lists, there were some doubtfuls. Party Whips were withdrawn. The decision was left to the free vote of the House.

Personally, I had no doubt as to how I wanted to vote. My difficulty was to decide whether or not I should vote at all in a matter affecting the Church of England.

The House was packed. There was electricity in the air. Archbishops and bishops, peers and commoners crowded the galleries. We were all keyed up. When the debate began, those who were in favour of the Revised Prayer Book declared that they had a majority of from thirty to forty. The opening was not particularly enthralling. It became tenser as "Jix" made the greatest speech of his life. There was a feeling then that we were going to decide great things. We wondered who was to be called upon next. After " Jix," there were several speeches rather more pedestrian, but such as would have been considered very good except for the comparison with the fine performance of Sir William Joynson-Hicks.

Many stood to catch the Speaker's eye on every occasion, among them my friend and colleague. His name was called. From the first sentence he held the House. In all my experience I have never seen a man dominate it so completely. There was not a movement on the benches or in the galleries. The voice ran up and down the scale. One moment it was a whisper. Another moment it was a bugle. The movements were intensely dramatic. When he said : " Then they cannot have this book," he thrust his hand forward. The House jumped. In twenty minutes he had ended with Luther's great phrase. The House heaved an audible sigh as the tenseness was relaxed. We knew that the business was finished. We had, for the first time, been right down to the heart of the whole controversy. That directness of speech which with the Greeks was a convention and with Glasgow men the expression of fearless opinion, had laid bare the true crux of the matter.

The speaker sat down famous. Great speeches followed on both sides. Then the vote, in an atmosphere of emotion and anxiety such as I have never known. The tellers marched into the House. " Against " was on the right. The cheers began. Members rose and waved their order papers. A minute's silence as the result was announced :

" For, 205 ; against, 247," and the cheering broke out again.

Then there was a rush for the Member for Paisley, but he was nowhere to be seen. As soon as he had known the result he had slipped out of the House. The whole British Commonwealth had watched that debate. That night the name of Rosslyn Mitchell was flashed over the world.

And now he and I, who had sprung from such diverse origins and had travelled a journey of a dozen years in closest friendship, were setting out for two months to the far ends of the world.

We were millionaires for two months. Yet, so strong were our traditions that, though we had fifty things to choose from at every meal, we continued our ordinary frugal life.

It would take a book to describe the wonders of that journey—the soft, kindly welcome of Quebec, the boisterous heartiness of Ontario, the prairie lands of Manitoba laden with grain, the prosperous stretches of Saskatchewan, the Rockies of Alberta and her wonderful National Parks, the fragrant fruit-lands of British Columbia, the wonders of buffalo, wapiti, bears and beavers, the mountains, glaciers, rivers and lakes. It was all new and wonderful, from the heat of the St Lawrence, as we entered, to the many-tinted maple-trees as we left Nova Scotia. What a world of beauty and wonder we crowded into those two months ! How small and yet how enticing was our little island home when we returned !

Our dwelling-place in Canada was the train, but much of our journeying was done by motor-car.

It came about that four of us travelled much to-gether : Sir Samuel Chapman, M.P. for South Edinburgh ; Sir Frank Sanderson, Bart., M.P. for Darwin ; Rosslyn Mitchell, M.P. for Paisley ; and David Kirkwood, M.P. for Dumbarton Burghs. There grew among us an intimacy that has remained one of the enriching phases of my life. I grew to love these men.

We were all politicians. We, Clyde men, were inclined to be dogmatic, fixed in our ideas and aggressive. They were politicians, but only part of the time. It was their training, the code again, the code of poise which, while it does not preserve them free from attack, leaves them unaffected by attack.

One of these men in answer to a phrase from me, " But what use is the Navy ? " replied in the most casual way :

" The Navy exists to prevent wars. When it cannot prevent them, it wins them."

To my ears that sounded boastful, but it was something more than that. It was a code, the code of a ruling class—indeed the code of a ruling race, casual but confident.

All my life I shall feel grateful to the Dominion of Canada for the glorious privilege of having seen their great country and for the knowledge which the visit gave me of the beauty of friendship.

Canada is not a country, it is a Continent. It has every form of natural beauty and natural awe that can be found in Europe. And it has among its ten million people members of every race in Europe. I went to a school in the prairie land where, among about fifty children, eleven

16

races were represented. In that little building race, language, and tradition of eleven countries were being moulded together to form the new type —Canadian.

However proud their parents may have been of England and Scotland and Ireland and Wales, of Russia and Poland and Germany and Greece and France and Finland, these youngsters were Canadians—and British. It was my first experience of a British nation across the seas. Wherever we went the Union Jack greeted us. At the luncheons and banquets which we attended the speeches were fervently British. Kipling's

> Daughter am I in my mother's house
> But mistress in my own

sums up the attitude of the Canadian people. I began to realize what deep meaning there is in the phrase : " A Free British People." Love of freedom for itself as a priceless individual possession, love of freedom of government as an independent people, were consistent with an equal love of Britain. It was as strong among the habitants of Quebec as among the Scots of Alberta.

In Toronto, where the atmosphere more nearly approximates to that of the United States, and where I found the strongest city-pride I have ever known, the emphasis on the British origin is as pronounced as in Nova Scotia, where I received a newspaper printed in Gaelic, the like of which we have not in all broad Scotland.

It may be that in Canada there is the nursery of a new race in which the blood of all races will be mingled. There seems no limit to the number of people that Canada can accommodate. She has ten million. She could have a hundred million. Her vast material resources are practically untouched.

We were told that an immense forest had been sold to a paper-pulp company. One of our group said, " I hope you insist on replanting."

" Well, sometimes we do," said our Canadian friend. " But this forest was burnt thirty years ago, and it will take the Company that length of time to cut down the timber which you see."

It is strange that, when travelling in a new country, the objects of interest which fill the guide-books are not the things that grip most strongly. All countries have their natural beauties. But just as visitors to Scotland are more interested in a few men wearing the kilt than in hills and glens and lochs, so I found myself fascinated by my first sight of a herd of buffalo and a meeting with an Indian Chief. They both happened at Banff, Alberta, a town bearing a name familiar to Scottish ears, and set in the heart of the Rocky Mountains. As I saw the herd of buffalo I was back to the days of my boyhood when Buffalo Bill and his Wild West Show visited Glasgow. And when I met Chief Sitting Eagle, a magnificent man who had studied agriculture at Toronto University and returned to live among his people, I remembered the many stories I had read as a boy in the Penny Dreadfuls against which we were warned and in which we found such pleasure.

One other thing attracted me greatly, to see

how a people can develop the tourist industry
without losing dignity. In Scotland, which is an
ideal country for the tourist, because it has so
much crammed into so little space, the tendency
is to regard the tourist industry as liable to make
the people servile. Whenever spring-time comes,
fervid journalists write articles on the evils of
encouraging tourists, as if the people of the Highlands and Islands sacrificed their independence by
entertaining strangers during three months of the
year. The Canadian has no such fear. He makes
it an industry. He accepts the stranger gladly,
even setting up notices outside of villages :
" Welcome to Woodville." In return for the
money the tourist brings, the Canadians set themselves to give him a thoroughly good time.

It was a wonderful experience to see in Canada
a land in the creation of whose prosperity men
and women of my race had played so large a part.
The Scots are a wandering folk. They have
spread all over the world. It may be because
they are so proud of their own country, and the
title of Scotsman, that they seem always to find
favour elsewhere.

CHAPTER XXII

Crisis and Change

I CAME home from Canada to find that we were nearing another general election. If I described it and what succeeded it, I should be repeating what I have said already. Labour was again the largest Party in the House. Labour was again His Majesty's Government. Ramsay MacDonald was again Prime Minister. Once more the lobbying and cajoling, the hopes and disappointments among those who sought office.

And once more, also, the absence of challenge. A Socialist Government cannot carry on a capitalist system better than the capitalists. The men bred by a capitalist system are men of affairs who understand their business. They are not apprentices.

It was the practice, and still is, for Socialist propagandists to refer to the great industrial magnates and their friends in the House as nonentities—stupid, cruel, selfish people who had fallen heir to positions of power which they have not the capacity to uphold. I have found that it is not so. The men in charge, whether in the world of industry or in the world of politics, are very able men. To change the system is a sound proposition. If those of us who wish to change the system can persuade a sufficient number of our fellow-citizens that a change is desirable, then a change will come. But merely to change masters is not worth striving for. If the system is to remain, I prefer that the men in control should be men who can do the job.

On one occasion I had publicly to repudiate

Caricature of the author, reproduced by courtesy of " The Evening News," Glasgow

a suggestion of an opposite nature. Sir Eric Geddes gave an address in St Andrew's Hall, Glasgow. My friend William Gallacher, the one unbending Communist in Scotland, interjected frequently. Sir Eric Geddes invited him to the platform and asked him to tell the audience frankly what he would do if he had power.

" The first thing I would do would be to give

Beardmore the sack and bring back David Kirkwood from Edinburgh and put him in charge." That was, in Glasgow phrase, "nonsensical." I felt bound to state in the Press that I had no sympathy with such an idea.

I am a craftsman. I think I am a better craftsman than ever was Sir William Beardmore. But I know no one who could have taken his place. He was a master. His mind was so made that he could supervise all the multitudinous crafts of that vast network of craftsmanship. A man may be a good craftsman and not a good shop steward, or a good shop steward without the capacity to be a good manager, or a first-class manager and a fourth-rate managing director.

It is one of the weaknesses of earnest Party politicians that they have the idea that, because a man is a good Tory or Socialist or Liberal, he is necessarily a good engineer or a good soap-maker. When I think of industrialists like Sir Thomas Bell, Sir John Hunter, Lord Weir, and Lord Invernairn—the name which hides Sir William Beardmore—I know that it is folly to think of suddenly catapulting other men into their place and expect them to do the job. An engineer serves a five-year apprenticeship. It takes twenty-five years to make an expert in management.

So with statesmen. Men of outside experience may become Members of Parliament and contribute valuable services to the State because of their outside experience. But the Baldwins, Neville Chamberlains and Churchills, the Ramsay MacDonalds and Snowdens, the Lloyd Georges, Simons and Runcimans are not evolved in a night like mushrooms. If they were, they would be mushrooms : very good mushrooms, no doubt, but there is a universe of difference between a statesman and a mushroom.

I cannot give any secrets about the collapse of the second Labour Government. I do not know the facts. Of one thing, however, I feel certain. If Ramsay MacDonald had come to a meeting of his Party and told them his views and invited them to join him in creating a National Government, most of them would have agreed. We all knew that national affairs were not going well. We had seen nations crash into chaos and had seen dictators rise to autocracy on the ruins. We were familiar with the idea of a non-party administration. Ramsay MacDonald had said on more than one occasion that he was willing to work along with any Party or any men, if by their combined efforts they could redeem the nation.

So strong was the hold that Ramsay MacDonald had on the Party in the House that, if he had come to the meeting, anyone who challenged him would probably have been howled down. The Clyde group were definitely antagonistic. They had lost faith in their leader. Others were opposed to coalition on principle. But they would have been swamped.

Instead, he sent Lord Sankey. He knew nothing of our Movement or of the working class. He made a poor show, talking to us like a benevolent old gentleman who carried peppermints in his jacket pocket to give to the poor workers. There was no kinship. He knew nothing of our demand for rights. He offered us a peppermint.

And there was no one there to say a word on behalf of Ramsay MacDonald and Philip Snowden and J. H. Thomas. They had stayed away. Their proxy was no good.

George Lansbury, Thomas Johnston, and other Ministers were there, but they had already made their decision and were silent. Only the Clyde men took an active part in the meeting.

The Clyde men had drifted far from Ramsay MacDonald and his Government. We had drifted from the Labour Party itself. But if one man of authority had spoken for Ramsay MacDonald and a National Government to meet a financial crisis, I believe he would have carried the Party with him. But there was none.

A friend of mine came back from Paris in July. He told me that he had heard in political circles there that we were to have a National Government. I did not believe it.

On August 1, 1931, a National Government was formed.

In November the country was thrown into the turmoil of a general election. What an election! I was terribly upset, more than tongue can tell, at the attack made upon the Labour Party by its former leaders.

Admitting that the Party had failed as a Government, it was Ramsay MacDonald, Philip Snowden, and J. H. Thomas who had been the three strongest leaders. But they blamed the rank and file. Some of us were worthy of blame. Our attitude had undoubtedly weakened the Government. But to attack the whole Party and the whole Movement was unjust.

The speeches of Philip Snowden made me think of a case in Glasgow where a man threw vitriol in the face of the girl he had jilted. It was inexcusable.

I was one of the few Socialists who retained their seats. Strangely enough, the little Clyde Group, aggressive and uncompromising, fared better than the others. But we also had lost our leader. John Wheatley, who was the finest brain among us and the best tactician, was dead.

The Labour Party came back, a mere remnant of its former greatness, to face a huge National Party whose leading men were our former leaders.

CHAPTER XXIII

The " Queen Mary "

CLYDEBANK and Dumbarton, the two burghs which I represent in Parliament, depend largely on shipbuilding for their prosperity.

For more than two years the Clyde had been like a tomb. Not a tomb newly made, but a tomb with a vast and inescapable skeleton brooding over its silence. For two years that gaunt framework had stood lifeless. It had sapped the vitality from a great town—aye, from a nation. Beneath its shadow men have crept about, battered and broken by enforced idleness.

These men—the finest, the most expert craftsmen in the world—had lived their lives in their work. Their joy as well as their livelihood lay in converting the vast masses of Nature's gifts into works of art, accurate to a two-thousandth part of an inch.

Workers in metal and wood, their brains and hands had become so well organized to work together that they could take the gigantic products of furnaces and rolling-mills and turn them into a thing of majesty and beauty. The highest talent of the sons of Tubal-cain, instructed of every artifice in brass and iron, was in their skill.

And yet, for two years and more, they had been shut out from the place of work and left idle in the street.

We think of prison as a place where men are shut in. It is worse than prison for men to be shut out of work.

And their wives—those heroic women of the tenement and the Guild—had seen their men depressed and nervous. They had long ago eaten up their little savings. They had struggled with untold splendour of sacrifice to pay the rent, to keep the husband and the children fed and clad ; aye, and still more to keep up the spirit of their men. To them the sight of the closed gate and the horrid framework beyond had been a blight.

Better a thousand times that the great ship had never been begun than that it should have stood mocking us all these weary months, dangling hope before hungry eyes and dashing faith to the pit of despair.

On Wednesday, December 13, 1933, the Chancellor of the Exchequer spoke a few sentences in the House of Commons.

As I looked across the green carpet and the Treasury table, I saw him, cool, detached, matter-of-fact. His sentences were as precise as the sentences of a judge. I heard him sentence Clydebank to Life.

There was one thing I wanted at that moment —a microphone to send a broadcast message to the Clyde :

" Men of the Clyde, lift up your heads ! "

And as I looked at him, juggling with the

happiness of thousands, I saw behind him the long Dumbarton Road through Clydebank with four thousand men moving along towards Brown's Yard while the horn sang out the morning welcome. I saw some whose pockets bulged with their ' pieces ' and some who would march out at dinner-time with a new ring in their step. These were the men who, years later, would tell their children :

" I worked on the ' 534.' "

Behind them I saw their homes, now so bare, gradually brighten with furniture and carpet and waxcloth, and children setting out for school, well fed and well clad. And I saw the wrinkles of care and anxiety smooth out from the faces of the mothers. And I saw the boys and youths eagerly awaiting the word " Go ! " to rush forward to begin the life that had so far been denied to them.

And beyond Clydebank I saw the glowing furnaces of Motherwell and Wishaw, the forges of Parkhead and the machine-shops and factories and wood-working yards of Glasgow. I saw the mines and the railways, the rolling-mills and the rivet factories full of energy and life. I saw engineers creating the giant turbines with 257,000 turbine blades.

I saw the anchors and the rudder, each weighing 140 tons. I saw the makers of glass preparing 2500 square feet of glass for side-windows and portholes. I saw the boiler-makers creating water-tube boilers of unprecedented accuracy with their 3000 feet of pipes. I saw gear casings weighing 200 tons and shaft brackets weighing 200 tons.

And I saw a shower of ten million rivets pouring down, each one to be fitted and welded with exact care. I saw weavers busy with carpets and linen ; cabinet-makers and upholsterers, joiners, carpenters, plumbers, electricians—all the craftsmen whose skill and industry have made the Clyde pre-eminent among the famous rivers of the world.

When Mr Neville Chamberlain announced that work on the great Cunarder " 534 " was to be resumed, I felt that the Clyde, one of the most depressed of areas in Britain, would become active again. And it was so.

As the skeleton took on flesh and lived again, Scotland revived. We are a nation of craftsmen. The whole world acknowledges our skill with admiration. This great ship which had depressed us began now to vitalize us.

Think of it ! The silence of years broke into the music of work. That grim, bare frame took on life and grew from hold to deck—four, seven, nine, eleven of them. Much of our depression had been mental. We had gone from bad to worse by thinking in terms of depression. Now, with " 534 " looming and growing, we began to throw off the chains of depression.

The " 534 " was our Statue of Liberty !

We had been battered, but we stood. The world had challenged us. We had not lost our soul. We had won through.

Our race had been through the most dreadful time in its history. We had borne our sorrows with dignity. We had kept the faith, that it was not intended we should disappear from the earth. And now we knew the Night was almost past. The Dawn already tinted the skies. We, too, were to have THE DAY—our Day, not of war and death, but of work and life.

For two years the skeleton in the yard of John Brown's had been an obsession to me. For two years I had written, spoken, pleaded, cajoled, threatened men and masters, shipbuilders and ship-owners, Cabinet Ministers and financiers. I outdid the importunate widow.

For more than two years " 534 " had been engraved on my heart. In the morning I woke wondering if something could be done that day to bring the skeleton to life again. During the day I made myself a nuisance to all and sundry. They said I had a bee in my bonnet. In the evening I would try to plan something new for the morrow.

That ship meant so much to me as a Scot. The Cunarders *Britannia, Lusitania, Aquitania,* were Clyde-built. With the " 534 " the Clyde was to top the world again. Britain was to hold again the sovereignty of the Atlantic.

I was utterly selfless in the agitation. I never thought of public opinion, whether for or against. I had set my heart on seeing that ship built, and all the determination and dourness in my nature rose to help me. My pertinacity was not resented. I was often put off, but I never suffered a rebuff. I admit I worried men. I annoyed them. I pestered them. Never once was I the object of unkindness or discourtesy. On the contrary, I was treated at first like a man with a mania. Then with sympathy. Then with encouragement. I talked with men whom I had never before met, many of whom had regarded me as a vehement and noisy partisan. They treated me as a confidant. During those two years I had to hold in my heart more secrets and confidences than in the whole of my life.

At last, having advanced stage by stage in the adventure, I carried my message to the highest in the land.

It is not good manners for one man to repeat a conversation he has had with another man. I have never done it, and I would not do it now, but for the fact that the talk I had with the Prince of Wales was an event of some importance not only to me, but to the men of the Clyde area.

It was Lady Astor who originated the idea. One night in the Lobby of the House she told me that the Prince of Wales was going to Scotland and wanted to have a talk with me about the conditions in the Clyde area.

In a flash I saw the vision of that gaunt and silent ship on the stocks at Clydebank, the most depressing sight in Great Britain of that day. I would do anything, go anywhere, plead with anyone if, by so doing, I could open that locked door for my Clydebank men.

But I refused Lady Astor's invitation. Why? I knew, when I had refused, that I was a snob. I had been to Sir Percy Bates, to Sir Thomas Bell, to the Prime Minister, the Chancellor of the Exchequer, Mr Walter Runciman, Sir Robert Horne, and a dozen other of the ' high heid yins.'

I began to wonder whether I was afraid to meet the Prince of Wales.

Then I received a formal invitation to Lady Astor's Reception " to meet H.R.H. the Prince of Wales," and the card said " Decorations." When I met Lady Astor, I had a joke with her about the " Decorations." The only decorations I had were my specs. When she asked me if I was coming, I told her I had no clothes but what I was wearing.

There I thought it ended. But an hour afterwards I was called to the telephone, and Lady Astor gave me this message :

" The Prince says it is not your clothes but yourself he wants to talk to, and, if you wear a serge suit, that is your best decoration."

There was a Robert Burns ring about that, man to man, Prince of the Realm and Engineer of the Forge—and behind it the thought of the great silent Cunarder. So I said : " Then I'll go."

At ten o'clock at night I was whirled away in a beautiful motor-car, a masterpiece of the engineer's craft. I had no idea what I was going to, and if I had been told I should have been no wiser. I knew nothing about a farewell dinner to the American Ambassador. I knew about the Cunarder.

I was received graciously, my hat and coat were taken, and I was led upstairs. Great doors opened and then it was an 'unco sicht.' Round a table sat about twenty people. In a flash I recognized the Prime Minister and Mr Baldwin and Lord Irwin.

Some one called "Mr David Kirkwood," and

17

everybody stood up. Before I had reached the
table, Lady Astor and the Prince of Wales had
walked round and welcomed me. It is funny how
the mind works, but the thing I remembered was
the engraving of Robert Burns in Edinburgh. We
walked a few steps, and the Prince said he was
very glad to have a chance of a talk.

" But we can't talk here," he said, " let's go
outside."

He took my arm and out we walked to a library.
Then the talk went like this :

" Well, how are things on the Clyde ? "

" Very bad."

" What do you think can be done ? "

" I want you to come down to Clydebank and
see the Cunarder. That ship means work. It
means life. It means the prestige of the British
Empire and the Blue Riband of the Atlantic."

" Well, tell me about it all."

" You want me to tell you the workers' point
of view without any varnish ? "

" Yes, no varnish, please."

" Well, sir, you have arrived on the scene at
the most momentous period in the world's history.
The heritage we have is what poets and dreamers
have talked about for ages. Man's ingenuity
applied to Nature has brought the age of plenty.
But, instead of plenty, we have reduction.

" It is not only the horny-handed son of toil
who has been reduced. It is everybody. The
result is an atmosphere of fear, and it has pene-
trated from the top to the bottom of Society, so
that those who are rich are curtailing expenditure.

" It has become fashionable to be economical. It used to be fashionable to be lavish. Every one is afraid to spend, rich and poor. Those who have wages are afraid to spend them. They are banking their money instead of spending it.

" It isn't only the workers who are hit. Do you know that there are in Scotland two thousand qualified school-teachers who have come through the Universities that we have no place for ? That is just one profession.

" For the young to-day there is no room in the inn. The Dominions, foreign lands, are shut. There is no outlet."

I was going on like this when I remembered Queen Victoria's description of W. E. Gladstone talking to her as if she were a public meeting. But the Prince of Wales egged me on. He said he wanted to hear all my point of view.

I told him what I would do if I were Chancellor of the Exchequer to increase the purchasing power of the unemployed. I told him 15*s.* 3*d.* a week was of no use. We could spend thousands of millions in a war, and if another war broke out we should do it again.

Why not spend money in a war against poverty ? After the Napoleonic wars there was a shortage. The trouble then was scarcity. To-day the trouble is abundance.

We went on for half an hour, when Lord Astor came to remind the Prince of the people upstairs. Then we started again, and I have never talked to any man in my life who was more eager to know just what the workers were thinking. So I told him how they viewed the production of wealth and their demand for the power to buy back what is produced.

Twenty minutes more passed in a friendly discussion. We were two British citizens talking about our land and our people. A man's a man for a' that. It was as if we were on a ship in a storm, when class and creed and caste are forgotten.

The Prince of Wales asked me to tell him what the people were thinking, the people I represent in Parliament, and I told the Heir to the British Throne what is thought in factory and workshop and on the street.

And I felt, as I feel when I see an expert engineer at work, that I had been in the presence of a man who has a big job to do, and is earnest and determined to do his job well. And what more can be asked of any man?

We went upstairs together and I was the spectator of a scene the like of which I had never witnessed. The numbers had increased to about two hundred. One by one, they were presented to the Prince. It was like a stage pageant. It was part of his job. In that part I was a stranger, but in the other part of the job I was a friend.

On Wednesday, September 26, 1934, the " 534 " was christened *Queen Mary* and launched into the River Clyde.

I first went to John Brown's shipyard as an engineer. That day it was as an engineer that I went to John Brown's shipyard. It was not as an engineer that I was invited. I was invited as Member of Parliament for the burgh.

Nearly forty years ago I had tramped the twelve miles from Glasgow to Clydebank seeking a job. I was a young engineer, eager as a race-horse, and taut as a wire rope.

I was proud of being an engineer. Every one on Clydeside knew that an engineer was a cut above other tradesmen. He was the aristocrat of the crafts.

Great factories were rising around Glasgow and ever-greater ships were building on the banks of the Clyde. In these, it was the engineer who was the mighty man. In his skill were power and beauty. In his heart burned ambition.

And there I was tramping to Clydebank, out of work. All along Clydeside were shipyards and engineering shops. They were busy, but they were full up. No one needed me, David Kirkwood, engineer, late of Beardmore's, Parkhead.

This day, my great day, had come. And with it came thousands of people to see King George V and Queen Mary launch the ship.

What a day ! The rain poured down in torrents —lashing, ceaseless rain. Across the river, on the other bank, great stands had been built for the spectators. Ships had brought to the yard thousands of distinguished guests who stood under an awning at the side of the ship.

Within a protected room, like a conservatory, there were gathered a few of the special guests. I was of the number. I looked through the windows and saw the men of Clydebank, thousands of them, standing in the rain, and I wondered what I was doing in the warm, covered conservatory. In the few minutes before the arrival of the King and Queen my memory flew back over the years and, like a man who is drowning, the whole story came back to my mind. It is the story as I have told it in this book. It is the story of a ruffled life, warm even to heat, disturbed, sometimes fretful, sometimes feverish. To any young men who ask me, I say always that politics and public affairs is by far the fullest and most interesting kind of life to lead. In it we touch the whole world. In it we support and develop our own corner of the world.

And on that day I felt that the whole nation was built into that ship. Throne and Parliament, Commerce and Industry, Arts and Crafts, parts of one great unity. And I remembered how in a former day this feeling had been expressed:

> This royal throne of kings, this sceptr'd isle,
> This earth of majesty, this seat of Mars;
> This other Eden, demi-paradise;
> This fortress built by Nature for herself,
> Against infection and the hand of war.
> This happy breed of men, this little world,
> This precious stone set in the silver sea,
> This blessed spot, this earth, this realm, this England.

But I wish William Shakespeare had said " this Britain " !

CHAPTER XXIV

Looking Backwards

THERE is nothing unusual in the saying: "This has been the most exciting half-century in the world's history." Every one, looking backwards, feels that way. He remembers events which excited him, novelties which appealed to his sense of wonder. The same events, described in a history-book, do not excite his children. The novelties of his youth are the normal experience of his children. They take all his realized dreams for granted. It is only their own dreams that excite them.

A Roman who had lived through the age that bore the stamp of Julius Cæsar might have said: "Never were such years in man's history." An Englishman who in his youth had watched the conflict between Cavalier and Roundhead through the reigns of Charles I and Cromwell, Charles II, James II, and William and Mary, from the attempted arrest of the Five Members of Parliament to the Massacre of Glencoe, could hardly help saying that his half-century had been the most exciting of all history. I am sure that to a Frenchman who was sixty years of age in 1835 no fifty years could appear more full of change and conflict than those of the Revolution and Napoleon, through which he had lived since he was ten.

We who live in an age of applied science think in terms of electricity, telephones, cinemas, wireless, motor-cars, aeroplanes, submarines, or, remembering that we are survivors of the Great War which sent the nations topsy-turvy, we may think in terms of monarchies and republics, dictatorships and the League of Nations.

Because I have lived my life among the ordinary people, artisans and labourers, I naturally take them as my test. What has the half-century meant to them ? Has it been exciting for them ? Has it made life fuller for them, or, what would have pleased them more, for their children and grandchildren ? I can best give my opinion in two pictures.

When I was a young apprentice women worked in the mills. I used to see them going to the mills at 5.30 in the morning. They were the girls of my station in life. They formed a miserable, pitiful procession. Their dress was a petticoat, a shoogan, and a plaid. They had no skirt, no coat, except the shoogan, which was a poor cotton jacket, the forerunner of the blouse. They had no hat, only the shawl thrown over their head. Because they had risen in the middle of the night to tramp along the long, dark road to their work, they were unkempt and unfed. Our women in Parkhead had boots. In other districts of Glasgow they went barefoot.

In these days I watch the same class of women leaving Singer's Factory in Clydebank. What a change ! There they are, neat and sweet with their well-cut tweed costumes, their fancy blouses, their dainty hats set on waves of well-trimmed hair. Look at the shoes and rayon stockings. That procession is a thing of beauty and has the fragrance of sweet soaps and the compactum. If in my youth a young woman had used powder she would have been chased for her life. Even to wear a hat was considered fast in a married woman ! They were doomed to drabness.

For release from the drabness women looked only to marriage, for it was then as now held to be humiliating for a wife to work in a factory. But it was little more than a change of drudgery. To-day, with houses that are a joy, and Guilds and cinemas and halls and happy dancing, a full life is available to the unmarried and married alike. They may not have much money, but they can spend it in palaces of merchandise. And beyond their cash wages is a social wage represented by health and unemployment insurance, maternity benefit, dental treatment, a more humane and therefore more scientific public assistance, old-age pensions, widows' and orphans' pensions, and a dozen other material benefits.

I have made the woman the mirror of the times, but man would reflect a similar change.

But the nearer approach of the artisan to the middle class does not stop at clothes and houses and food and entertainment. It is as obvious in social life. Class-distinctions are fast losing their importance as the standard of judgment. Intelligence and character are the tests to-day. Snobbery has almost gone. Religious prejudice is passing. Political prejudice has gone. We cannot conceive of a situation such as John Morley was placed in when, desiring to introduce James Keir Hardie to William Ewart Gladstone, he was politely but firmly told that the introduction would not be acceptable to the great leader of Liberalism.

And I am not seeking to deny that this improvement has taken place in a capitalist society. I have never accepted the theory of a " Dying Capitalism." So long as a capitalist society can adjust its laws and its conventions to meet the developing sense of justice and reason of the people, it will continue. It continues to live, like the stag, by shedding its antlers. My satisfaction lies in seeing the process of development approximating to the Socialist outlook. In fact, capitalism is surviving only in the measure of its acceptance of the Socialist outlook.

I have been called a heretic and a rebel. I am both. I have seen many of my heresies accepted and many of my revolutionary ideas adopted in various spheres. I have a great many more in my mind that have not yet been accepted or adopted. I may live to see them adopted yet.

It was to me a terrible shock, on going into the workshop, to find men who were regarded outside as saints show themselves mean, underhand, cruel, and selfish ; to find them foul-mouthed and often drunken. It is not so to-day. There may be fewer who are called saints, but there are many more who deserve the title. I have protested against the preaching of " fire and brimstone " and the " miserable worm " conception of humanity. I have denounced superstition and sanctimoniousness. In my youth we had many " Holy Willies." How rare they are to-day, and in what universal contempt they are held !

I have seen the churches of this and other lands outstrip the barrack-yard for brutality and bloodthirstiness. I have known Germans, French, Austrians, and the rest. I have seen them in their own lands. I protested against the ecclesiastical denunciation of them as devils. And I have seen the whole Church change its attitude and become a messenger of peace instead of a Moloch of war. I have seen this nation, which gave to the world the most terrific example of tenacity and ferocity in arms, become the very heart of the movement for peace among all peoples.

The path of the rebel and the heretic is not an easy path to travel. The scorn and often the assaults of his neighbours is not pleasing to any man. I have seen Ramsay MacDonald and Philip Snowden and a host of other men tread that path. I have walked that way myself. Some who set out in our company have been broken on the journey. Some have been driven into themselves and become cynical and arrogant, so that every statement they make is a snarl. But those who have kept their souls and gone on have found that those who hated them have learned to respect them. And in that change has come a wider tolerance and a deeper understanding.

There is much for the rebel and the heretic to do. We have still much injustice and much superstition, but we now know that the major injustices are fading and that reason is winning. In the process, dislocation of material things and mental outlook is inevitable, just as in the industrial world every new mechanical invention dislocates hand-labour. Yet I refuse to believe that man, whose inventive skill conceives the machine, will allow the machine to master his mind and bring ruin where it offers riches. I believe that plenty will yet be accepted by man as the cure and not the cause of poverty, that political leaders will yet adjust the laws of industry and the customs of the people to the demands of new circumstances and conditions. I believe that character and moral power will eradicate the numbing influence of superstition and myth.

The heretic, who always appears as the enemy of the Church, has proved to be the giver of life. So the rebel who appears to be the enemy of society is in reality its saviour.

> Man hath all that Nature hath and more,
> And in that more lies all his hope of good.

When the mind and heart of men are trained to use the ' more,' they will find Nature a bountiful friend of all.

Whatever changes I have seen, great as they are, are incomparably smaller in extent and in quality than those which we are yet to see. The Conservative of to-day would regard the proposals of the Liberals of my youth as altogether inadequate and, indeed, has expanded them in a multitude of ways.

It seems to me that the true work of the rebel
against injustice is not to cause unnecessary and
harmful disorder, but to show to the people where
injustice exists, to convince them that it need not
exist. When he has succeeded in doing that,
others will remove the injustice and claim the
honour of doing so. They are welcome to
it.

There are still injustices, vices, and vulgarities
in the world. War and poverty I see already
marked down for destruction. The vice of drunken-
ness is going. Even the motor-car is at war with
strong drink. Gambling, which is a fearful blight
on the workers to-day, will pass as people grow
in intelligence and life grows in interest. The sin
of intolerance is nearing its dissolution. I find
to-day a kindlier spirit and a more generous attitude
among men than I have ever known. Although
religious leaders complain of the lack of interest
in religion, the ethical standard is higher than it
has ever been.

It is a mad world in many ways, but a glad
world in more. There is a vast luxury in being
alive in these times when thought is battering at
the gates of prejudice. There is a magnificent
opportunity for great venturing in untracked areas
of politics and economics, in national harmony
and international understanding.

And beyond the fever of city strife and political
struggle there are the sun and stars and sea, and
" Nature's charms, the hills and woods, the sweeping
vales and foaming floods," and birds and beasts
and flowers, and music and art and books to

read, and, above all, man and maid and little children.

> Then let us pray that come it may
>   (As come it will for a' that),
> That Sense and Worth o'er a' the earth,
>   Shall bear the gree, an' a' that.
> For a' that, an' a' that,
>   It's comin' yet for a' that,
> That Man to Man, the world o'er,
>   Shall brothers be for a' that.

It is a gladsome thing to have lived during the past sixty years, and a still gladder prospect to be spared for the next twenty, to watch the world that the new generations are creating for their successors from the elements of the world which we created for them.

I would not change the road I have come, though often it was my fate to walk alone. But the journey is not over. The New Road beckons. I know I shall not be alone, because so many who would not walk with me before are at my side as good companions for the journey.

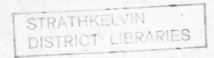